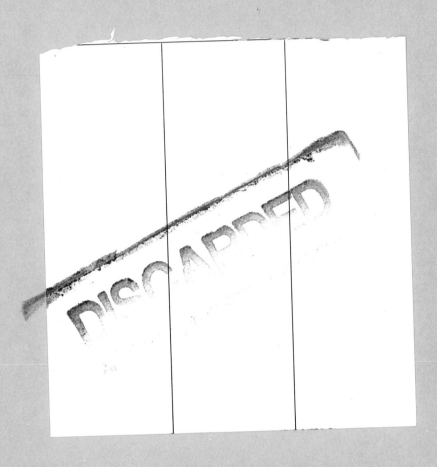

A GARDENER'S GUIDE TO

Bulbs

Editor Jane Courtier

Series Editor Graham Strong

INDEX

CONTENTS

KEY TO AT A GLANCE TABLES

PLANTING   FLOWERING

At a glance tables are your quick guide.
For full information, consult the accompanying text.

ABOVE: Tuberous begonias come in a glorious range of colours.

LEFT: Brilliantly coloured tulips are, for many people, the epitome of the spring and early summer season.

GROWING BULBS

Bulbs are the easiest of plants to grow – probably no other plant group gives as much variety and pleasure to the gardener with so little effort. Even people without gardens can enjoy bulbs as there are so many that make excellent container plants.

Most people think of bulbs as an essential part of spring, but spring is by no means their only season – there are bulbs that flower through the summer, autumn and even through the depths of the winter. They are usually very easy to look after, and many types will go on giving pleasure for years with the minimum of attention.

ABOVE: These parrot tulips just breaking from their buds already show the typical ruffled petals and colour streaking.

LEFT: Deepest blue hyacinths make a wonderful foil for the bright yellow tulips in this landscape planting.

BULBS, CORMS, TUBERS AND RHIZOMES

What most people know as bulbs covers a whole range of plants with some kind of underground storage organ that allows their survival over their dormant season, which may be winter or summer. They include true bulbs and plants with corms, tubers and rhizomes.

• True bulbs are made up of a bud enclosed by modified leaves or fleshy scales from which roots and shoots emerge. The shoots grow out of the pointed top and the roots from the other end. Most, such as onions, daffodils, and hyacinths, have an outer papery cover or tunic: lilies, which are bulbs, too, have a bulb of swollen leaf bases but lack the protective tunic.

• Corms are bulb-like structures formed by the enlargement of an underground stem base. They do not have the 'rings' of true bulbs, but stems grow out of the top and roots from the base in the same way. Freesias, gladioli and crocuses all grow from corms.

• Tubers are swollen underground parts of roots or stems. Dahlias grow from buds at the ends of tubers.

• Rhizomes may grow underground or along the soil surface. They are fleshy, tuberous roots with new growth emerging from the end. Some irises grow from rhizomes (other irises are bulbs). Some bulbous plants described as having rhizomes or tubers appear to have little more than a small crown from which the roots emerge.

For convenience, all the above groups are discussed throughout this book as bulbs.

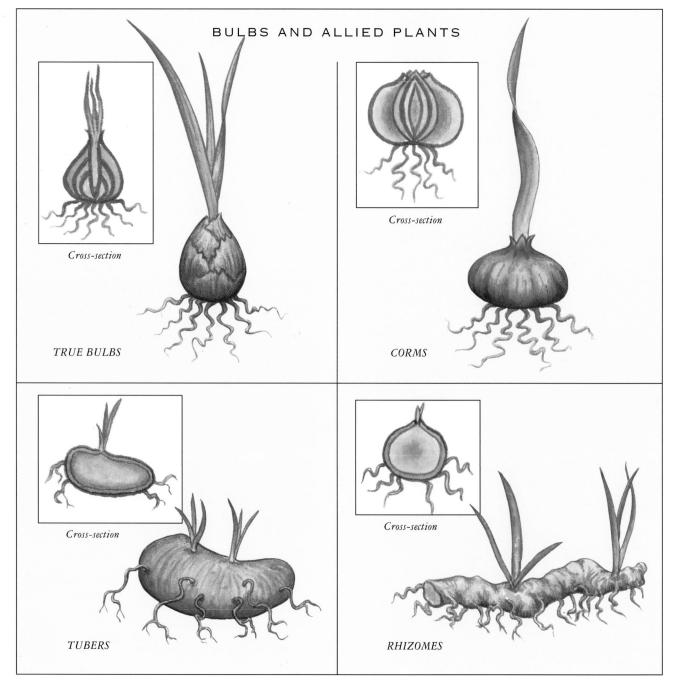

BULBS AND ALLIED PLANTS

Cross-section

TRUE BULBS

Cross-section

CORMS

Cross-section

TUBERS

Cross-section

RHIZOMES

TENDER BULBS

Indoors or out?

Some bulbs are not suitable for growing outdoors in our climate, and must be grown in a greenhouse or conservatory, or in the home, to produce good results. In many cases, bulbs can be started into growth under protection and brought outside later in the season when the weather has warmed up: when grown in containers, these look good on patios or even positioned amongst other flowering plants in borders so that the container is hidden. Other bulbs, however, need to be grown under protection throughout their lives, as their flowers would be spoiled outdoors.

Which bulbs must be considered tender enough for indoor cultivation often depends on the area in which you live, and the situation of your own garden. Species that can be grown successfully outside in the mild South-west of the country would often fail in cold, exposed Northern gardens, but even in mild regions a garden may be exposed to chilly, windy weather that makes it unsuitable for the more tender plants.

Experience is often the only way to gain an accurate picture of which plants are hardy enough for your conditions, but when growing dubiously hardy bulbs, always play safe and overwinter one or two specimens under cover in case an unexpectedly cold winter destroys your outdoor stock. Protect slightly tender bulbs by heaping straw, dry leaves or bracken over the planting site once the foliage has died down in autumn: this helps to prevent frost penetrating to the bulbs below ground. Deep planting is also recommended for extra protection.

The table below gives a guide to the plants that need indoor conditions, and those that are risky outdoors in all but the most favoured areas of the country. It is often adequate to bring tender bulbs under cover for the winter only: the information under each bulb entry gives further details.

THE TUBEROUS ROOTS of dahlias can be left in the ground in some areas, but are better lifted and stored in a frost-free place.

TENDER BULBS

BULBS FOR THE HOUSE, GREENHOUSE OR CONSERVATORY ONLY

- Achimenes
- Clivia
- Gloriosa
- Hippeastrum
- Lachenalia
- Sinningia

BULBS NEEDING PROTECTION OR OVERWINTERING UNDER COVER IN COLD AREAS

- Agapanthus
- Amaryllis
- Canna
- Crinum
- Cyrtanthus
- Dierama
- Eremurus
- Eucomis
- Gladiolus callianthus
- Hedychium
- Hymenocallis
- Ixia
- Nerine
- Polianthes
- Romulea
- Schizostylis
- Sparaxis
- Sprekelia
- Tigridia
- Tritonia
- Zantedeschia
- Zephyranthes

AGAPANTHUS PLANTS are suitable for leaving outdoors over winter in warmer areas of the country only.

STRONGLY CONTRASTING white and rich crimson tulips are mass planted under a silver birch tree in this lovely garden. The tulip planting is brilliantly set off by the wide, sweeping border of purple Virginian stock.

CHOOSING BULBS

What do you want from your plants?

There are so many bulbs, in such a range of colours, sizes and forms, that it is all too easy to get carried away when buying them. Their appeal is instantaneous: here they are, ready packaged, just needing to be popped into the soil – and within a short time, with no further effort, you can expect to be enjoying the brilliant flowers pictured on the display units at garden centres.

Perhaps one of their greatest virtues is that the bulk of bulbs appear for sale at just the time when summer is finally drawing to a close. The summer flowers are nearly over, trees will soon be shedding their leaves and the days growing shorter and more gloomy; the cold, wet, miserable weeks of winter stretch out ahead. No wonder we are so pleased to see the arrival of bulbs, with their promise of the spring to come!

But in order to achieve the best possible results from your bulbs, you should plan for them more carefully. Consider the type of garden in which they are to be grown; whether it is mild and sheltered or cold and exposed. Where in the garden are the bulbs to grow? Is there space on a rock garden or in a border? Do you have an area of lawn where bulbs could be naturalised, and if so, are you prepared for the grass to be untidy while the bulb foliage is dying down? Do you want all your bulbs to flower in spring, or would a longer flowering season be more appropriate? Do you want bulbs in pots for growing on the patio, or varieties that will flower out of season to brighten up the home in the middle of winter? If you have a good idea of what you want from your bulbs *before* you go out to buy them, it could save you making some expensive mistakes.

Choose for colour

Consider the colour schemes of your bulb planting as you would any other item, either inside your home or outside it. Do you want strong contrasts in colour, gradations of a single colour or colours that complement each other? Do you want to create a bright, warm, active look or do you want to give a cooler, calmer impression? Warm, active colours are red, yellow, orange and bright pink, while blue, lavender, white, cream, pale pink and pale yellow are cooler colours.

Blue and white spring-flowering bulbs include spring star flower, grape hyacinth, bluebell and hyacinth, all of which would team well with white or cream daffodils. Some of the brightest bulbs in the 'hot' colour range are ranunculus and harlequin flowers (sparaxis). Both these are more commonly available in mixed colours but sometimes you can find a supplier who is able to sell them as single colours. Anemones also come in strong colours and these too can be purchased in single colours. Greater impact is generally achieved by planting blocks of single colours rather than mixtures. Try bulbs in blocks of red, orange and yellow for a tremendous impact, or if you want a quieter look, plant groups of two shades of pink and white.

Many bulbous plants, such as daffodils, come in a wide range of varieties but a fairly limited colour range: they also look their best if planted in groups of one variety. Corn lily is another good example. Although there is a wide colour range available and corn lilies can be purchased in mixtures, these flowers look best if planted in blocks of one colour. They can, of course, be planted as mixtures, especially in an informal garden setting, but in nature they would be more likely to grow in blocks of one colour.

Consider flowering time

Some gardeners prefer one huge display over three or four weeks in spring while others may find more interest in spreading the season over several months of the year. For instance, with crocus alone, different varieties provide blooms from late autumn right through to mid-spring. There is some form of bulbous plant to give a display in every month of the year if that is what you require.

It can be hard to give precise information on exactly when different species will be in bloom, as the time can vary from one district to another and even from one garden to another because of variation in microclimates. However, if you spend some time noting the times when bulbs flower in your garden, in future seasons you will be able to plan to have a succession of bulbs in flower during many months of the year.

BUYING BULBS

There are several different ways in which you can buy bulbs. Most garden centres, and several other stores, sell bulbs in perforated plastic bags backed by a card giving planting details, along with a picture of the bulb in flower. Bulbs are also available in small netting sacks with attached pictures and growing instructions. Most garden centres and nurseries sell bulbs in bulk in the main planting season, and you can make your own selection from large bins. Another option is to send away for catalogues from bulb-growing nurseries and order bulbs by mail – these growers advertise in popular gardening magazines. The range of bulbs available from specialist nurseries is generally very much more extensive than what is on offer at your local garden centre. Mail order is a good option if you want some of the more unusual varieties, and if you want to order a lot of bulbs as it can be a good deal cheaper, though you need to take postal charges into account. When planning to buy by mail order, remember that you need to order well in advance of the planting date; if you leave it until bulbs are starting to appear in the shops, the specialist suppliers are likely to have sold out of many of the less common varieties. Once you are on the mailing list of mail order suppliers, they will send you their catalogues in plenty of time in future years.

When buying bulbs at a garden centre, try to buy them as soon as possible after they have been delivered, as they tend to deteriorate in the warm conditions, and will soon become bruised as other buyers sort through them to make their choice. Select plump, firm, well-rounded bulbs and make sure there are no soft spots or patches of mould. Especially avoid buying any bulbs that are starting to shoot and showing signs

HYACINTH BULBS will be on sale from early autumn. Select yours early to be sure of getting the best available.

GOLDEN DAFFODILS planted in sweeping drifts beneath a fine magnolia tree show to advantage against an old stone wall.

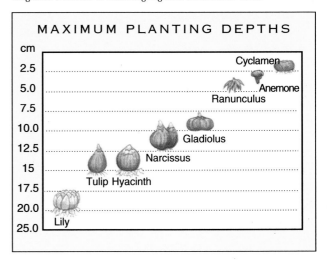

MAXIMUM PLANTING DEPTHS

cm
2.5 .... Cyclamen
5.0 .... Anemone
Ranunculus
7.5
10.0 .... Gladiolus
12.5 .... Narcissus
15 .... Tulip Hyacinth
17.5
20.0
25.0 Lily

GROUPS OF BRIGHT PINK, autumn-flowering nerines provide showy splashes of colour as summer flowers fade.

BLUEBELLS, TULIPS and daffodils are here planted informally in a lovely woodland setting beside a tiny stream.

of growth. Unless there is just the tiniest shoot appearing and you know you can plant the bulbs at once, these bulbs will be a bad buy as they will not thrive. Some chain stores and supermarkets sell bulbs and continue to display them long after they should have been planted out or discarded. If you see long pale shoots emerging from bulbs definitely don't buy them. These bulbs have been stored for too long in poor conditions. They are badly stressed and have used up a great deal of their stored reserves of energy and growing capacity so that they may fail completely or do very poorly. Try to make your selection early in the season so that you have a choice of the best on offer.

Bulbs are best planted as soon as possible once you get them home, but if you are forced to delay planting for a short while, store the bulbs in paper bags or nets – not plastic bags – and keep them in a cool, dry, airy place. If the weather is very warm, the crisper drawer of a refrigerator can be a good place to keep bulbs in good condition, but do not put them in the main part of the refrigerator as this will dry them out.

PLANTING BULBS

Choosing a site
For the majority of bulbs, choose an open planting site where they will receive sun for at least half a day. There are a few bulbs that will grow well in shade but most like at least some sun. Even woodland species such as bluebell and wood anemone grow as understorey plants in deciduous woodlands and so receive some sun during their early growing and flowering period, before the trees are fully in leaf.

The vast majority of bulbs need well-drained soil or they will rot. If there is any doubt about the drainage, plant bulbs

in raised beds or mix sharp sand or grit with the soil in the planting area. Bulbs like a fairly rich, fertile soil. At least a month before planting, incorporate a generous amount of well-rotted manure or garden compost into the planting area.

Positioning the bulbs
Your bulbs will look more natural if you plant them in clumps or groups, not in straight lines. The depth depends on the size of the bulb but it is usually two or three times its diameter (see diagram on page 9). Details of planting depths are given in the individual entries for each bulb, and refer to the depth of soil above the tip of the bulb. Spacing between bulbs is also dependent on size. Larger bulbs are usually set out about 8cm (3in) apart and smaller ones 2–5cm (1–2in) apart, but they can be crowded together for effect.

Be sure to plant the bulbs the right way up. Usually the pointed part points upwards, but there are exceptions to this rule: ranunculus and anemone have the claws or points facing down into the soil and some lilies and crown imperials are sometimes planted on their sides to avoid moisture collecting between the scales, which can lead to rotting.

In dry conditions, bulbs may need to be watered in after planting, but it is usually not necessary to water again at least until leaf shoots have appeared.

Planting under trees
Mass planting of bulbs that flower through winter and early spring under deciduous trees can turn what might otherwise be a somewhat dull area of the garden into a lovely feature. Although it is sometimes difficult to dig and plant in these areas as the soil is hard and full of matted roots, the result can be well worth the effort. The leaves that fall from the trees in autumn break down into leafmould which provides ideal growing conditions for the bulbs.

MAJESTIC WHITE LILIES grown in a large ceramic container make a stunning decoration for a courtyard.

INCREASING YOUR STOCK OF BULBS

Left to themselves, many bulbs will multiply of their own accord, but there are a number of ways in which you can help the process along.

Separation
Many bulbs produce offsets or bulblets that can be gently broken away from the mother bulb when the bulbs are lifted, and planted separately. Most first-year bulblets will reach flowering size in two or three years if they are planted separately, but some are slower to flower. When separating clumps of dahlia tubers, make sure each tuber has an 'eye' attached or it will not sprout and flower.

PROPAGATING DAHLIAS

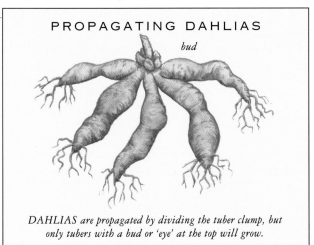

bud

DAHLIAS are propagated by dividing the tuber clump, but only tubers with a bud or 'eye' at the top will grow.

THREE WAYS TO PROPAGATE LILIES

1 DETACHING SCALES

THE LILY BULB consists of lots of scales. Remove the outer scales.

PUSH the individual scales, right way up, into a box of moist peat.

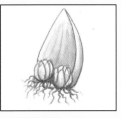

BULBLETS will appear at the base of each scale.

POT UP the scales when the new bulblets appear.

2. DETACHING AERIAL BULBILS

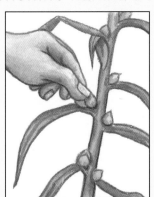

BULBILS grow in the leaf axis of some species. Collect them and pot them up.

3. DETACHING BULBLETS

OFFSETS on the base of some lilies can be detached and planted out.

LIFTING BULBS

1. *PUT A FEW STAKES around the edge of the clump so that you know where to dig when the leaves have died down.*

2. *AFTER THE LEAVES have died down, use a spade to outline the area of the clump.*

3. *LIFT THE CLUMP UP with a fork and shake off as much soil as possible.*

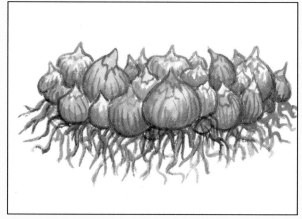

4. *SEPARATE THE BULBS from the clump, clean them and then store them in a dry, airy place or replant them.*

Scoring and scooping

Cut a V-shape into the base plate of a mature bulb at planting time, taking care not to damage the growth bud of the bulb. This should result in many small offsets being produced by the end of the growing season. Or score through the basal plate of the bulb at right angles with a sharp knife to produce the same result. Depending on species these small offsets should produce bulbs of flowering size in two to four years.

With a sharp-sided teaspoon or curved knife, you can scoop out the entire basal plate and bulblets will form around the rim of the scooped out area. Wear gloves if you are treating hyacinths as the sap can sometimes irritate the skin.

Lilies

These techniques are not suitable for lilies, which are propagated by other methods (see page 11).
• A mature lily bulb is composed of numerous individual scales. The individual scales can be carefully removed and planted upright in a coarse, free-draining mixture such as three parts coarse washed sand and one part peatmoss or peat substitute. The scales should produce bulblets at their bases.

• Some lilies produce aerial bulbils in the axis of the leaf and these can be collected as they are about to fall. Potted into pots or trays they should produce leaves by the following spring and reach flowering size in two or three years.
• Other lilies produce bulblets just below the soil surface, around the base of the stem. If these are carefully dug out from among the roots they can be potted up and will form flowering plants in two or three years.

CARING FOR GROWING BULBS

Once planted, bulbs need little maintenance. Once the plants are actively growing, the soil should be kept moist, but never soggy. Bulbs do not usually need feeding before they flower. They are fed after blooming, when they are storing food for the following season's growth. Special instructions for feeding and watering are included in the entries for individual plants where appropriate.

AFTER FLOWERING

• After flowers have finished, cut off the spent flower stems but do not cut back the foliage. If you cut off the leaves before they have died down naturally, the bulb will not have the reserves to grow and flower the following season.

• After flowering, feed the plants with a liquid or granular balanced fertiliser and continue to water in dry conditions until the leaves begin to die off naturally. This may take about two or three months.

• If bulbs have been planted in clumps, you may be able to plant annuals between the clumps, using either seed or seedlings. Quick growers such as Virginian stock will provide a pretty distraction from the dying bulb foliage. You could also put in summer-flowering annuals or perennials that will be ready to take over the display once the bulbs have truly died down. Or you can, of course, purchase some 'potted colour' – annuals that are already in bloom.

• Bulbs do not usually need to be lifted every season. Most are left in the ground and lifted only every two or three years, or in a number of cases only every four or five years. Many bulbs flower well when they are crowded and then it is only necessary to lift and divide clumps when the flower numbers or quality drop off.

• Take care when you lift bulbs that you do not cut or damage

TALL WHITE RANUNCULUS dominate this white border, formed of plants with contrasting shapes, textures and sizes.

A CARPET OF COLOUR has been created in this garden bed by combining white tulips with violas and anemones in a range of colours. To achieve such a pleasing effect, careful planning before planting is necessary.

TALL BEARDED IRIS make an elegant border for this attractive garden path. Irises come in a rich array of colours.

ZEPHYR LILY, with its starry white flowers and deep green glossy foliage, makes an ideal edging plant. Here it grows with portulacas.

them – it is easy to slice into them with a spade or spear them with a fork. Discard damaged, soft or rotted bulbs immediately. Place the sound bulbs to dry in a cool, airy spot, brush off excess soil and then store them in nets, old stockings or in single layers in cardboard boxes. Ideally, bulbs should be stored so that they do not touch each other: they can be kept separate with shredded paper or something similar.

• Because lilies have no protective outer sheath on their bulbs, they must be lifted, the clumps divided if necessary and the bulbs replanted at once. They can be stored for short periods in damp sphagnum moss but take care that they don't dry out.

• Some bulbous plants, such as freesias, produce quite a lot of seed if the spent flower stems are not cut off. You can collect these seeds when they are ripe or allow them to self-sow. Seedlings may take two to five years to reach flowering size, depending on the type of bulb, and they will probably not be true to type. The results can, however, be interesting as you never know quite what to expect. Particularly good seedlings should be marked at flowering time so that the bulbs can be propagated at the end of the season.

MAKING THE MOST OF BULBS IN THE GARDEN

You may wish to plant groups of bulbs under deciduous trees or in other permanent places in the garden but there are many other options. Bulbs mix well with many herbaceous perennials as the new growth of the perennials tends to camouflage the not-so-attractive foliage of the bulbs as it yellows and dies off. Bulbs in this situation can usually be left in the ground for several years before they need to be lifted and divided.

Many bulbs can be treated like annuals for a seasonal display, then lifted and stored for use the following season. This, of course, creates more work but the results can be well worth the effort, allowing you to create different displays each year. You can have a delightful show of bulbs on their own but consider the possibility of planting bulbs and spring bedding plants together for a really stunning spring display. As well as forming an attractive association, the bedding plants help to mask the dying foliage of the bulbs, which must be left to die down naturally if the bulbs are to flower well next season. Autumn-sown hardy annuals will also serve the same purpose. Plant your bulbs and bedding plants at the same time, placing a bulb between each of the plants. For best effect, planting should be quite dense. You can experiment with colour combinations or opt for tried and tested associations such as yellow lily-flowered tulips and blue forget-me-nots.

• An early-flowering bedding plant such as white primula could be interplanted with cream or yellow narcissi, or deep blue anemones for a vivid contrast.

• White, yellow-centred primulas would team well with blue *Anemone blanda* and the dwarf narcissus 'Tête-à-Tête'.

• Other spring-flowering plants to combine with bulbs include polyanthus, wallflowers and forget-me-nots.

Dwarf bulbs are ideal for growing on a rockery, usually providing colour and interest before the other alpine plants come into their own. Suitable bulbs include alliums, chionodoxa, crocus, cyclamen, iris, muscari, narcissus, oxalis and rhodohypoxis, among others.

IF YOU WANT show quality tuberous begonias, grow them under cover. Here they grow in a conservatory, where they can also be placed on raised benches so the flowers are more easily admired.

NATURALISING BULBS IN GRASS

Bulbs naturalised in grass make a very attractive feature in gardens. However, you need to remember that the bulb foliage must be allowed to die down naturally if the bulbs are to perform well in future years, and that means that the grass cannot be mown for several weeks after the bulbs have finished flowering. This can look rather untidy, so a position for naturalised bulbs needs to be chosen with some care. Popular sites are the perimeters of lawns or under deciduous trees. In a small garden with a limited area of lawn used for many purposes, naturalising in turf may not be a practical idea.

Choose bulbs that will flower at an appropriate period; early spring is convenient because the grass can then be mown from late spring onwards. Some summer-flowering bulbs are good in a wildflower meadow, and autumn-flowering bulbs such as colchicum also grow well in grass. You can either lift a square of turf, plant a group of bulbs and replace the cut turf, or you can plant larger bulbs individually, using a trowel or bulb-planting tool to cut a hole in the turf. Place the bulb in the bottom of the hole and replace the plug of soil and turf. Give a good watering after planting, both to settle the bulbs and to help the turf re-establish.

After the bulbs have bloomed, give the plants an application of balanced fertiliser and water the area regularly if conditions are dry. Once the bulb foliage has yellowed and died off mowing can be resumed – this usually takes some six weeks after flowering.

MINIATURE PINK NERINES and other small bulbous plants grow between paving stones where they benefit from the sharp drainage.

GROWING BULBS IN CONTAINERS

Many bulbs make lovely container plants. Pots full of bulbs are ideal for balcony gardens and patios, and for instant colour, pots of bulbs in bud or in flower can be plunged into garden beds throughout the growing season.

Use a good quality potting compost, and make sure the base of the container is crocked for good drainage. Plant the bulbs at the same depth as you would in the soil, crowding them into the container for a good flowering display. Keep the compost moist at all times; regular watering will be needed.

Growing bulbs indoors

'Prepared' bulbs are specially treated to flower early – often in time for Christmas. Plant them in a shallow pot or bowl of moist potting compost and put them in a cold place such as a garden shed, keeping them dark by placing them in a black plastic bag. Leave them for 8–12 weeks; when shoots begin to appear, move them into a bright, cool room. Once flower buds begin to show colour, move the bulbs to their flowering position in the home.

The bunch-flowered narcissus 'Paperwhite' is unusual in that it doesn't need a cold, dark period after planting; bulbs can be left on a cool, light

A POT OF JACOBEAN LILIES can be brought to the fore when they flower.

POTTING NARCISSI FOR INDOOR USE

1. CHOOSE A POT at least twice as tall as the bulbs.

2. HALF FILL the pot with a good soilless potting compost.

3. POSITION THE BULBS with their tops level with the top of the pot and a small gap between each and around the edge of the pot.

4. COVER THE BULBS with the compost and gently firm it down. Water, drain and place in a cold – 4°C (40°F) – position in total darkness. A cold, dark period of 8–12 weeks is necessary.

5. WHEN SHOOTS appear, move the pot into a bright, cool position at about 10°C (50°F).

6. WHEN BUDS appear, move the pot into its flowering position, still in bright light.

WHAT CAN GO WRONG?

There are relatively few pest and disease problems that regularly beset the home gardener growing bulbs. Bulbs that fail to come up at all have usually been planted too deep or have rotted through disease or waterlogging, especially in clay based soils. Yellowing foliage early in the growing season may also be caused by waterlogging. More serious pests of bulbs are often associated with storage conditions and it is wise to examine bulbs for damage, decay or insect pests such as aphids before planting. Diseases specific to certain bulbs are mentioned in the text under individual entries.

Failure to flower
This may be due to a number of reasons, including:
• natural offsets are not sufficiently mature to flower.
• foliage has been cut off prematurely the previous season.
• insufficient sunlight or lack of water while the foliage is still green.
• congestion of bulbs.
• 'blindness' – a condition that occurs especially with daffodils and tulips. The flower bud forms but gives up trying to continue on to bloom. It may be due to incorrect storage temperature, lack of chilling or fluctuating temperatures as the flower bud emerges from the bulb.

Leaf scorch
• This fungal disease affects bulbs of daffodils and narcissi, and others including hippeastrum, crinum and belladonna lilies. It is worse in wet seasons, and occurs at the top of the bulb scales so that emerging leaves are infected. The leaf tips are reddish and scorched, and later on brown spots appear further down the leaf. Eventually the tissue around these damaged areas goes yellow. Remove and destroy the worst affected leaves and spray with a suitable fungicide if symptoms persist.

Bulb rots
• These may be caused by a number of bacteria or fungi, and lead to rotting and decay of the bulbs either in store or in the ground. They are made worse by poor drainage and overwet soil conditions. Damaged bulbs are particularly prone to infection, so take care when handling or lifting bulbs and discard damaged ones.

Grey mould (botrytis species)
• Grey mould attacks an enormous range of plants. It may manifest itself initially by spotting on leaves or stems, followed by breakdown of the tissue and the typical furry grey growth. Poor air circulation, overcrowding, overwatering and cool, humid weather conditions are favourable to its spread. Improve growing conditions and spray if necessary with a suitable fungicide.

Bulb flies
• Bulb flies lay their eggs in the soil near the bulb neck; the maggots tunnel into the bulb to feed. Affected plants produce sparse, yellow foliage and fail to flower. If you are not lifting the bulbs in autumn, pull soil up round their necks to fill the holes left by the leaves dying down.

Thrips
• Gladioli are very susceptible to attack by thrips, or thunderflies. These tiny winged insects cause silver streaking and flecking of both foliage and flowers; in a bad attack, the display can be ruined. The pest is worst in hot, dry conditions. Affected plants can be sprayed with a contact insecticide. Thrips overwinter on the corms, so after an attack, dust the corms with HCH dust after lifting and again before planting out in spring.

Lily beetle
• These small, scarlet beetles can be a serious pest of lilies and other plants such as fritillaries. Both larvae and adults feed on the leaves and stems of plants, often causing considerable damage. They are quite conspicuous and should be picked off by hand and destroyed whenever they are noticed; bad infestations can be sprayed with a contact insecticide. Beetles overwinter on weeds and plant debris, so clean up round the planting area in autumn.

Aphids
• These may attack a range of bulbous plants and should be sprayed or hosed off as they can carry virus diseases. A bad infestation disfigures flowers and foliage.

MULTI-COLOURED RANUNCULUS and anemone are crowded together to produce this bright springtime scene.

Continued from page 16
windowsill directly after planting and flowers will appear in
about six weeks. Plant mid-November for Christmas blooms.

Normally, non-prepared bulbs will flower at their normal
period. They should be planted and left out in a sheltered
position in the garden in their containers until flower buds
are showing, when they can be brought into the house.

After flowering

If after flowering the whole plant and bulb are planted out
into the garden, there is some chance of the bulb flowering
the following year. Bulbs that stay in their pots until
they have died down will in most cases not reflower the
following year. When the foliage on these bulbs has died
down, lift the bulbs, store them and replant them in the
garden at the right time the following season. They may not
flower that year but should do so the next. They are not
suitable for growing as indoor-flowering plants again.

BULBS AS CUT FLOWERS

Many bulbous plants produce flowers that are ideal for
cutting for the house. Most are best picked before they are
fully open. For longer vase life, change the water daily or add
a few drops of household bleach, or a proprietary cut flower
food to the water.

*FRAGRANT FREESIAS come in a glorious range of colours to
epitomise the joy of the spring garden.*

THIS RUSTIC BASKET of choice hyacinth blooms could not fail to lift the spirits, appearing as they do just when winter draws to a close.

TULIPS MAKE ideal cut flowers and several colourful bunches are here shown to perfection against the terracotta of the containers.

ACHIMENES
Hot water plant

HOT CERISE PINK flowers decorate this pretty little plant throughout summer. Hot water plants come in a range of colours.

THE LARGE, delicate purple-blue flowers of Achimenes *'Paul Arnold' help to make this one of the most popular varieties.*

FEATURES

Achimenes are easy to grow and undemanding; they are raised from small rhizomes that look a little like miniature fir cones. Leaves are toothed, elongated and slightly furry in texture, and the colourful, trumpet-shaped flowers are carried in profusion on short stems above the foliage. The plants often assume a semi-trailing habit, making them good for growing in a basket, or in a raised pot where the stems can cascade.

Flowers are available in a wide range of shades including cream, pink, red, purple and blue; some varieties have attractively veined throats. Although individual flowers are quite short lived, they are quickly replaced by a profusion of others throughout the season. The plants grow to about 25cm (10in).

ACHIMENES AT A GLANCE

A colourful house and greenhouse plant, flowering throughout the summer. Minimum temperature 10°C.

		RECOMMENDED VARIETIES
JAN	/	
FEB	plant 🖐	'Little Beauty'
MAR	plant 🖐	'Paul Arnold'
APR	/	'Peach Blossom'
MAY	/	'Queen of Sheba'
JUN	flowering 🌸	
JULY	flowering 🌸	
AUG	flowering 🌸	
SEPT	flowering 🌸	
OCT	/	
NOV	/	
DEC	/	

CONDITIONS

Aspect   Bright light is necessary, but not direct sun, which may scorch the foliage and flowers.

Site   House plant, preferring cool to moderately warm conditions without marked temperature fluctuations. Use soilless potting compost, based on peat or peat substitute.

GROWING METHOD

Planting   Bury the rhizomes shallowly – about 2cm (⅜in) deep – in a pot of moist compost, spacing them about 1.5cm (½in) apart, in early spring. Keep the pot in a warm room.

Feeding   Feed with a high potash liquid fertiliser every 10 days or so from when the flower buds appear. Keep the compost just moist when the rhizomes start to grow, increasing the watering slightly as flowers start to form, but ensure the compost is never saturated. Tepid water is preferred, hence their common name. Stop watering when the flowers have faded.

Problems   No specific problems, though aphids may attack the new growth.

FLOWERING

Season   Flowers profusely throughout the summer.
Cutting   Flowers are not suitable for cutting.

AFTER FLOWERING

Requirements Stop watering once the flowers have faded and allow the plants to dry off. Remove the dead top growth and keep the rhizomes in the pot of dry compost over winter in a frost-free place. The following spring, tip them out, pot them up carefully in fresh compost and water to start them into growth again.

AGAPANTHUS
African lily

THE BLUE AND WHITE *flowering heads of agapanthus are each composed of numerous individual flowers.*

THIS DENSE PLANTING *of agapanthus needs little attention and yet rewards the gardener with its wonderful summer flowers.*

FEATURES

Usually sold as perennials, agapanthus have showy heads of bright blue, trumpet-shaped flowers. Their foliage is deep green and strap shaped, forming a rosette; the stout flowering stems arise from the centre in mid-summer. Several species are available, but they all like a sheltered spot – in cold gardens, they can be grown under cover in a greenhouse, being moved outside in warm summer weather. 'Headbourne Hybrids' are the most widely available; flowers may be several shades of blue, or white. They are deciduous, reasonably hardy, and grow from 60–120cm (2–4ft). *Agapanthus umbellatus* (*A. africanus*) is evergreen with purple-blue flowers, but most plants sold under this name are in reality *A. campanulatus*, a deciduous species with blue or white flowers to 90cm (3ft).

AGAPANTHUS AT A GLANCE

Stately plants with eye-catching, rounded heads of blue flowers. Best in warmer gardens.

		RECOMMENDED VARIETIES
JAN	/	
FEB	/	'Headbourne Hybrids'
MAR	/	'Bressingham Blue'
APR	plant	
MAY	plant	
JUN	/	
JULY	flowering	
AUG	flowering	
SEPT	flowering	
OCT	/	
NOV	/	
DEC	/	

CONDITIONS

Aspect A sheltered position in full sun is required.
Site Usually best grown in tubs or large pots on a sunny patio. Suitable for reasonably sheltered gardens only: can be grown in a conservatory or greenhouse in cold areas. Plants need free-draining soil with plenty of organic matter such as well-rotted garden compost. In containers, use loam-based potting compost with extra organic matter added.

GROWING METHOD

Planting Plant the fleshy roots 10–15cm (4–6in) deep in late spring. Take care not to let the roots dry out before planting.
Feeding Apply a high potash liquid fertiliser occasionally during the growing season; container-grown plants should be fed every 14 days. Keep the soil moist but never waterlogged through the growing season; do not let plants in pots dry out at any time.
Problems Plants may fail to perform well in exposed gardens, otherwise they are generally trouble free.

FLOWERING

Season Flowers from mid to late summer.
Cutting Stems may be cut when the lowest flowers on the globe-shaped head are opened, but they are better enjoyed on the plant.

AFTER FLOWERING

Requirements Allow the leaves of deciduous varieties to die down and cover the crowns with a layer of straw to protect them during the winter months. In cold areas, move the plants under cover until spring.

ALLIUM
Ornamental onion

LARGE ROUNDED HEADS are typical of alliums and the star-burst effect of this one looks stunning in the garden.

THE PURPLE-PINK FLOWERS of Allium oreophilum (also known as A. ostrowskianum) brighten up the early summer garden.

FEATURES

There are a large number of *Allium* species, including edible onions, garlic and chives as well as many ornamental plants. Typically, they produce rounded heads of flowers, often in rosy purple shades, but there are also yellow and white-flowered species. Some are small-growing and suitable for the rock garden, while others make excellent plants for the middle or back of borders. *A. giganteum* produces its eye-catching heads of mauve-pink, starry flowers on stems 1m (3ft) or more high, while *A. moly* grows to only 20cm (8in) and has loose clusters of golden yellow blooms. Many alliums make excellent cut flowers. They are usually long lasting in water, and the dried inflorescence which remains after the blooms have fallen can be used successfully in dried arrangements, too.

ALLIUM AT A GLANCE

Versatile and varied bulbs with usually rounded heads of starry flowers in spring and early summer.

		RECOMMENDED SPECIES
Jan	/	
Feb	/	*Allium albopilosum*
Mar	/	*A. beesianum*
Apr	flowering	*A. caeruleum*
May	flowering	*A. giganteum*
Jun	flowering	*A. karataviense*
July	flowering	*A. moly* 'Jeannine'
Aug	/	*A. neopolitanum*
Sept	plant	*A. oreophilum*
Oct	plant	*A. schubertii*
Nov	/	*A. siculum*
Dec	/	

CONDITIONS

Aspect Best in full sun but will tolerate light shade.
Site Alliums in borders should be positioned where other plants will help to hide their often untidy foliage. Smaller species are suitable for rock gardens. The soil must be well drained and should contain plenty of well-decayed manure or compost. Add a dressing of lime to acid soils before planting.

GROWING METHOD

Planting Plant in autumn. Planting depth varies according to the size of the bulb: cover bulbs with soil to three times their height.
Feeding Apply a high potash liquid fertiliser as buds form. Water during dry spells, but never allow the soil to become sodden. After flowering, stop watering altogether.
Problems Plants may suffer from the fungal disease rust, causing orange pustules on the foliage: destroy affected specimens. Feeding with high potash fertiliser may increase resistance to attacks.

FLOWERING

Season Flowers in late spring and summer.
Cutting Cut alliums when about half the flowers are fully open.

AFTER FLOWERING

Requirements Foliage starts to die down before blooming is complete. Cut off the spent flower stems if required. Overcrowded clumps can be divided in autumn, replanting immediately.

ALSTROEMERIA
Peruvian lily

THE FLOWERS of alstroemeria are very delicately marked when viewed close-up, and have an almost orchid-like appearance.

SUMMER BORDERS are brightened by these colourful, long-lasting flowers which are also excellent for cutting for the home.

FEATURES

These exotic-looking plants are prolific flowerers which can be spectacular in borders. The open-faced flowers are carried in clusters at the top of 90cm (3ft) stems; the sword-like foliage is dark green. The plants may take a year to become established and produce flowers, but once they have settled in, flowering is profuse. Container-grown plants become established more quickly. The colour range includes yellow, cream, orange, red, salmon and pink. The Princess series contains dwarf varieties that represent a major breeding breakthrough. Alstroemerias are from South America and are not always reliably hardy; Ligtu hybrids are among the hardiest types.

ALSTROEMERIA AT A GLANCE

Once established, these plants produce a profusion of colourful, attractively marked summer flowers on tall stems.

		RECOMMENDED VARIETIES
JAN	/	
FEB	/	
MAR	plant 🌱	Ligtu hybrids
APR	plant 🌱	Princess series
MAY	/	
JUN	flowering 🌸	
JULY	flowering 🌸	
AUG	flowering 🌸	
SEPT	/	
OCT	/	
NOV	/	
DEC	/	

CONDITIONS

Aspect   Full sun or partial shade.

Site   Alstroemerias do well in a sheltered border and are very effective mixed with herbaceous perennials. They require free-draining soil.

GROWING METHOD

Planting   Plant the fleshy tubers 15cm (6in) deep in spring, as soon as you obtain them. Handle them carefully, as they are usually brittle and break easily. Do not let them dry out before planting. You can also obtain alstroemerias as container-grown plants in summer.

Feeding   Add a balanced granular fertiliser to the soil before planting. Water plants in very dry conditions, but never allow the soil to become waterlogged.

Problems   Plants may fail to flower in their first season after planting. Once established, however, they can be very invasive, and should be planted where their spread can be kept in check. Slugs find them attractive, and should be controlled with slug pellets where necessary.

FLOWERING

Season   Flowers in mid-summer.

Cutting   Alstroemerias last very well in water, and should be cut as the buds start to open.

AFTER FLOWERING

Requirements   Remove dead heads. Once the foliage has died down, protect the crowns with a mulch of dry straw or leaves through the winter. Crowded clumps can be split in spring.

AMARYLLIS BELLADONNA
Belladonna lily

THESE TALL FLOWER STEMS appear before the leaves, which is why belladonna lilies are also known as 'naked ladies'.

BRIGHT PINK BELLADONNA LILIES brighten the late summer and autumn garden. The foliage here is from a clump of daylilies.

FEATURES

This lovely South African bulb produces its multiple and sweetly perfumed blooms on sturdy purple-green stems 60cm (24in) or more high. The funnel-shaped flowers may be various shades of pink or white and the flowering stem appears before the leaves, giving the plant its alternative common name of naked lady. This bulb is a great asset in the garden as the flowering period is autumn, while the glossy strap-like leaves look good throughout winter and early spring. It makes an excellent cut flower. Best flowering comes from clumps that are left undisturbed for several years.

AMARYLLIS AT A GLANCE

A tall plant producing its stems of fragrant, funnel-shaped flowers in autumn. Needs a warm, sheltered, sunny position.

		RECOMMENDED VARIETIES
JAN	/	
FEB	/	'Johannesburg'
MAR	/	'Kimberley'
APR	/	'Major'
MAY	/	
JUN	plant	
JULY	plant	
AUG	/	
SEPT	flowering	
OCT	flowering	
NOV	/	
DEC	/	

CONDITIONS

Aspect   Prefers a warm, sheltered spot in full sun – the bulbs need a good summer baking to produce the best flowers.

Site   A good plant for a flower bed under a south-facing wall. *Amaryllis belladonna* can also be grown in containers, planting the large bulbs singly in 20cm (8in) pots. Well-drained soil is required: poor soil is tolerated but best results are achieved by digging in decayed organic matter a month or more before planting.

GROWING METHOD

Planting   Plant bulbs with their necks just at ground level and 20–30cm (8–12in) apart in early to mid-summer.

Feeding   Apply a balanced fertiliser after flowering, as the leaves appear. Water in dry periods while the plant is in growth.

Problems   It is rarely troubled by any problems.

FLOWERING

Season   Flowers in very late summer and autumn.
Cutting   A good cut flower for large arrangements.

AFTER FLOWERING

Requirements   Remove spent flower stems. Protect the crowns with a mulch of peat over winter. Leave bulbs undisturbed for several years. If lifting and dividing, do so in early summer.

ANEMONE
Windflower

THE DARK CENTRES, deep blue or black, of Anemone coronaria make a stunning contrast to the rich colours of the petals.

THIS MIXED PLANTING of Anemone coronaria shows some of the range of colour and form available from this lovely plant.

FEATURES

Anemones, also known as windflowers, form a large and versatile group of plants, the most commonly grown species being *A. coronaria*, *A. blanda* and *A. nemorosa*. *Anemone coronaria* grows from a hard little tuber, *A. blanda* from hard tuberous roots and *A. nemorosa* from very brittle, creeping rhizomes. The flowers are often very colourful, and can be daisy-like with lots of petals, or cup-shaped, rather like poppies. Anemones flower in spring; *A. coronaria* will also flower in summer, depending on the planting time. They are excellent for cutting.

ANEMONE AT A GLANCE

Low-growing, hardy plants which form a colourful carpet of spring or summer flowers.

JAN	/	
FEB	flowering 🌿	
MAR	flower 🌿/plant 🌿 *	
APR	flower 🌿/plant 🌿 *	
MAY	/	
JUN	flowering 🌿	
JULY	flowering 🌿	
AUG	flowering 🌿	
SEPT	plant 🌿 **	
OCT	plant 🌿 **	
NOV	/	
DEC	/	

RECOMMENDED VARIETIES

Anemone blanda:
 'Atrocaerulea'
 'White Splendour'
 'Radar'
Anemone coronaria:
 'Mona Lisa'
 'Mister Fokker'
Anemone nemorosa:
 'Alba Plena'
 'Purity'
 'Robinsoniana'
 'Vestal'

* summer flowering   **spring flowering

TYPES

A. coronaria Reaching 15–20cm (6–8in) high, *A. coronaria* is available in a lovely range of clear colours including red, white, blue, violet, cerise and pink, all with a black to deep navy blue centre. The most popular strains are 'de Caen', with single poppy-like flowers, and 'St Brigid', with semi-double to double flowers. There are many named cultivars in both these strains. They can be planted in single blocks of colour or mixed at random, and they can be grown in containers as well as making an excellent garden display.

A. blanda This native of Greece and Turkey bears daisy-like flowers, usually in shades of blue, although white and pink forms are available. One of spring's early bloomers, its flowers are carried on stems some 15–25cm (6–10in) high above ferny, divided leaves. A variety of cultivars is available now and some of these are grown as potted plants. This species seeds readily and can be naturalised under trees.

A. nemorosa The wood anemone, *A. nemorosa*, likes a cool, moist climate and is often grown massed under deciduous trees, imitating its natural habitat. Here, its starry, white (sometimes lavender blue), single flowers, with their central boss of golden stamens, make a glorious showing in late spring and into early summer. The wood anemone's mid-green foliage is deeply cut. Growth may be from 10–20cm (4–8in) high. This species increases rapidly where it finds the growing conditions suitable, and plants will eventually increase to carpet the ground.

THE BRIGHT, DAISY-LIKE flowers of Anemone blanda *brighten up the garden in late winter or very early spring.*

*WOODLAND ANEMONE (*Anemone nemorosa*) makes a pretty groundcover in a cool, moist climate where it naturalises readily.*

CONDITIONS

Aspect All anemones prefer some protection from strong wind. *A. coronaria* is best in full sun, while *A. nemorosa* prefers to be grown in dappled sunlight or with morning sun and afternoon shade. *A. blanda* comes from exposed sites in mountainous districts and so will tolerate full sun or part shade.

Site *A. blanda* and *A. nemorosa* grow well under deciduous trees, or on a rock garden, while *A. coronaria* provides bright colour towards the front of beds and borders. Soil must be well drained or tubers and roots will rot. All anemone species prefer a soil rich in organic matter although *A. blanda* is happy to grow in fairly poor soils as long as drainage is good. Plenty of well-decayed compost or manure should be dug into the ground about a month before planting the bulbs.

GROWING METHOD

Planting Plant tubers of *A. coronaria* 5cm (2in) deep and 10–15cm (4–6in) apart in September and October for spring flowers, or in March and April to bloom in summer. *A. blanda* and *A. nemorosa* should be planted 5–7.5cm (2–3in) deep and 10cm (4in) apart in early autumn. Take care not to damage brittle roots; soaking the tubers or rhizomes overnight before planting will help them to get established quickly. After planting, mulch soil with bark chips or leafmould.

Feeding A balanced fertiliser can be applied after flowering, but feeding is not usually necessary in reasonably fertile soils.

Water in after planting if the soil is dry, and ensure the soil is kept moist but not waterlogged once the flower buds start to form.

Problems Mosaic virus can cause distortion and mottling of the leaves and eventual death of plants. Control aphids, which spread the virus.

FLOWERING

Season *A. coronaria* will bloom from late winter until mid-spring, or in mid- summer, depending on planting time. *A. blanda* flowers in early spring while *A. nemorosa* flowers later in spring and into early summer.

Cutting *A. coronaria* makes an excellent cut flower. Cut rather than pull flowers from the plant. The flowers of *A. blanda* and *A. nemorosa* may last a few days in the vase but these anemones make a much better showing in the ground. Leaving the flowers on the plants allows seed to form to increase your stock.

AFTER FLOWERING

Requirements If dry, continue to water plants until the foliage dies down. Cut off spent flowerheads unless you require seeds to form. Tubers of *A. coronaria* can be lifted, cleaned and stored in a dry, airy place until the following autumn, or left in the ground as long as drainage is good. The other species are best left in the ground to form large colonies. Lift, divide and replant in autumn if required.

ANOMATHECA

Syn. *Lapeirousia laxa*

THE OPEN-FACED, trumpet-shaped flowers resemble those of freesias, and are carried on slender spikes above the foliage.

THESE PLANTS may well be quite small, but the bright colour of the flowers really stands out in the garden, even when seen from a distance.

FEATURES

Occasionally known as scarlet freesia, this pretty little plant is trouble-free and most rewarding in the garden. It multiplies readily from seed sown in spring. The trumpet-shaped flowers are pale scarlet with darker markings. They appear in mid-summer and are followed by seed pods which split open to expose red seeds. The slightly stiff, ribbed, sword-shaped leaves grow about 15–20cm (6–8in) high while the flowers are held on spikes which extend well above the foliage. There is a pure white cultivar, 'Alba', but this is not nearly as vigorous as the species. *Anomatheca viridis* has unusual green flowers and is normally grown as an indoor plant, flowering in early spring.

ANOMATHECA AT A GLANCE

A graceful, pretty bulb with sprays of trumpet-shaped flowers. Reasonably hardy in most areas.

JAN	/	
FEB	/	
MAR	/	
APR	plant 🌱	RECOMMENDED VARIETIES
MAY	/	
JUN	/	*Anomatheca laxa:*
JULY	flowering 🌼	'Alba'
AUG	flowering 🌼	'Joan Evans'
SEPT	flowering 🌼	
OCT	/	*Anomatheca viridis*
NOV	/	
DEC	/	

CONDITIONS

Aspect — Grows happily in full sun or partial shade.

Site — This bulb is very useful for the front of borders, or for growing in pots for the patio or in the house or conservatory. Ideally, soil should be well drained but it need not be rich.

GROWING METHOD

Planting — Plant corms about 5cm (2in) deep and the 10cm (4in) apart in spring.

Feeding — Supplementary feeding is generally not needed, but on poor soils a balanced fertiliser can be applied after planting. Plants in containers should be given a liquid feed every 14 days throughout the growing season. In very dry springs, water occasionally once plants have started into growth.

Problems — No specific pest or disease problems are known for this plant.

FLOWERING

Season — Flowers generally appear in mid-summer.

Cutting — This is not a good choice as a cut flower.

AFTER FLOWERING

Requirements — Cut off faded flower stems immediately after flowering if you do not want seed to set. In warm gardens the corms can be left in the ground, but in cooler areas they are better lifted in autumn and stored for replanting next spring.

BEGONIA
Begonia

EXQUISITE FORM and beautiful colour shadings make this tuberous begonia a show stopper. It's worth the effort to produce blooms like this.

THE LARGE, many-petalled flowers of some begonia hybrids are reminiscent of camellias. This variety is 'Roy Hartley'.

FEATURES

Tuberous begonias result from the breeding and selection of several South American species and many are grown by specialists for exhibition. *Begonia tuberhybrida* is the most commonly grown type; the hybrid 'Non-Stop' strain is particularly popular for its prolonged flowering. Begonias make excellent house plants, but can also be grown in containers on patios or in beds outdoors; pendulous varieties are especially suitable for hanging baskets. Flowers can take many forms, including single or double, camellia-flowered or carnation-flowered – some are very simple while others are heavily ruffled. Flowers appear in threes, with the large, central male flower being the showpiece; the small female flowers are usually removed as they develop. The colour range includes many shades of red, pink, yellow, cream and white, with some bicolours. Plants grow some 25–45cm (10–18in) high.

BEGONIA AT A GLANCE

Very large, showy flowers are carried throughout the summer. Plants are frost-tender.

		RECOMMENDED VARIETIES
JAN	/	
FEB	/	'Billie Langdon'
MAR	plant (under cover)	'Can-Can'
APR	plant (under cover)	'Fairylight'
MAY	plant (under cover)	'Orange Cascade'
JUN	plant (outside)	'Roy Hartley'
JULY	flowering	'Sugar Candy'
AUG	flowering	
SEPT	flowering	
OCT	/	
NOV	/	
DEC	/	

CONDITIONS

Aspect   Begonias prefer dappled sun or light shade, and need shelter from wind.

Site   Grow the plants in the house or conservatory, or in pots or flowerbeds outdoors once all risk of frost has passed. Soil should be rich and moisture retentive, with plenty of organic matter such as well-rotted garden compost.

GROWING METHOD

Planting   Dormant tubers can be started off in pots of moist peat or compost under cover in spring, pressing the tuber into the soil with the dished side up. Spray the top of the tuber once only with a fine mist of water, and keep the compost just moist. Pot-grown plants can also be bought in leaf later in the spring. Plant out when all risk of frost is over, 23–30cm (9–12in) apart.

Feeding   Apply high potash liquid fertiliser every 14 days throughout the growing period. Keep the plants moist at all times, but do not allow the soil to become waterlogged.

Problems   Powdery mildew may be a problem, especially in hot, dry weather. If this occurs, try to improve air circulation round the plants and use a suitable fungicide if necessary.

FLOWERING

Season   From early summer right through to autumn.

Cutting   Flowers are unsuitable for cutting.

AFTER FLOWERING

Requirements Lift tubers as the stems die down in autumn. Store them in dry peat in a cool, frost-free place until the following spring.

CAMASSIA
Quamash

The intense blue flower spikes of Camassia leichtlinii make a striking group amongst other border plants. A moisture-retentive soil is needed for best results – regular watering is likely to be necessary if the weather is dry. Camassias can cope with heavier soil conditions than many other bulbs.

FEATURES

The botanical name of this plant is derived from that given to it by American Indians, who grew the bulbs for food. It is relatively unusual among bulbous plants in preferring moist, heavy soils. The tall, graceful flower stems carry dense spires of starry blue flowers. *Camassia leichtlinii* is very reliable, with 1m (3ft) flowering stems: *C. quamash (C. esculenta)* is a little shorter and has flowers varying from white, through pale blue to deep purple. *C. cusickii* produces its 1.2m (4ft) pale lavender flower spikes in late spring.

CAMASSIA AT A GLANCE

Tall, stately spikes of blue, starry flowers provide valuable colour in the perennial border in early summer.

		RECOMMENDED VARIETIES
JAN	/	
FEB	/	*Camassia cusickii*
MAR	/	
APR	/	
MAY	flowering	*Camassia leichtlinii:*
JUN	flowering	'Electra'
JULY	flowering	'Blue Danube'
AUG	flowering	'Semiplena'
SEPT	plant	
OCT	plant	*Camassia quamash*
NOV	/	
DEC	/	

CONDITIONS

Aspect   Full sun or light, dappled shade will suit these bulbs.

Site   Camassias make excellent border plants, valuable for early summer colour. A moisture-retentive, fertile soil is preferred, though they will also grow adequately in free-draining conditions.

GROWING METHOD

Planting   Plant the bulbs in early to mid-autumn, 7.5–10cm (3–4in) deep. Space them about 15cm (6in) apart.

Feeding   Feeding is not usually necessary, but an application of a balanced, granular fertiliser can be made in spring, especially on poor soils. Water thoroughly in dry conditions and on free-draining soil.

Problems   Camassias are usually trouble free.

FLOWERING

Season   Flowers from late spring through early summer.

Cutting   Stems can be cut as the lowest buds on the spike begin to open.

AFTER FLOWERING

Requirements   Cut down the flowering spikes once the flowers have faded. Do not disturb the bulbs until they become overcrowded, when they can be lifted and divided in autumn.

CANNA
Indian shot

THE APRICOT-ORANGE FLOWERS of these cannas will contribute a rich, flamboyant colour to the garden for many months.

THE COLOUR of these scarlet cannas is highlighted by the darker green, slightly bronzed foliage that surrounds them.

FEATURES

Canna is an exotic-looking plant with bold, brilliantly coloured flowers carried on tall stems, up to 1.2m (4ft), above large, paddle-shaped leaves. The large blooms form an impressive spike; colours available are mainly shades of yellow, orange and red. Sometimes the flowers are bi-coloured, or spotted, streaked or splashed with a contrasting shade. The foliage is also attractive, and in some varieties is tinged with bronze or purple. There are a number of varieties with attractively variegated foliage, which has yellow or pink veins.

Cannas are not hardy and must be protected from frost. *Canna indica* is the best known species, but most varieties generally available are hybrids, often sold as *Canna hybrida*. A wide range of named varieties is available from specialist suppliers.

CANNA AT A GLANCE

An impressive, exotic-looking plant with tall stems of brightly coloured flowers and lush, attractive foliage.

		RECOMMENDED VARIETIES
JAN	/	
FEB	/	'Durban'
MAR	plant (indoors)	'Lucifer'
APR	plant (indoors)	'Oiseau de Feu' ('Firebird')
MAY	plant (outdoors)	'Picasso'
JUN	plant (outdoors)	'Wyoming'
JULY	flowering	
AUG	flowering	
SEPT	flowering	
OCT	/	
NOV	/	
DEC	/	

CONDITIONS

Aspect These plants must have an open but sheltered position in full sun.

Site Cannas make an impressive focal point in a bedding display, in mixed or herbaceous borders, or grow well in tubs and large containers. Soil should be free draining but rich in organic matter. In cold areas, the plants are best grown in a greenhouse or conservatory.

GROWING METHOD

Planting Set the rhizomes about 7.5cm (3in) deep in fertile soil in late spring, once the risk of frosts is over. Better plants will be obtained by starting the rhizomes off in pots in a frost-free greenhouse in April, and planting them outide in early summer, once all risk of frost is over and the weather is suitably warm.

Feeding Give an occasional high potash liquid feed as the flower buds develop. Keep the soil moist at all times but make sure that it is never waterlogged.

Problems No specific problems are generally experienced.

FLOWERING

Season Flowers in mid to late summer, until the first frosts.

Cutting Flowers are not suitable for cutting – they are best enjoyed on the plants.

AFTER FLOWERING

Requirements Lift and dry the rhizomes in early autumn, before the first frosts. Store them in a cool, frost-free place in just-moist peat or sand through the winter. If kept bone dry, the rhizomes will shrivel.

CHIONODOXA
Glory of the snow

'PINK GIANT', *a variety of* Chionodoxa siehei, *has relatively large blooms in a pale, purplish pink shade.*

THE BRIGHT BLUE *flowers of chionodoxa, with their prominent central white eye, make a cheerful sight in the early spring months.*

FEATURES

This dainty little bulb is ideal for rock gardens or raised beds, with its mass of open, star-shaped blue flowers with white centres. They are carried on short spikes of up to a dozen or so flowers per spike. The strap-shaped leaves form loose, rather untidy rosettes.

Chionodoxa luciliae (C. gigantea) grows to 10cm (4in) tall with clear blue, white-eyed flowers some 4cm (1½in) or more across. *Chionodoxa siehei,* which used to be known as *C. luciliae,* and is sometimes listed as *C. forbesii,* reaches 10–25cm (4–10in), with slightly smaller flowers which are available in pale blue, white or purplish pink forms. The flowers have a distinct white eye and a central boss of stamens, tipped with gold. *C. sardensis* has flowers of a striking gentian blue with a tiny white centre that is almost unnoticeable.

CONDITIONS

Aspect Full sun or dappled shade is suitable, though they grow best in an open, sunny position..

Site Chionodoxa is suitable for window boxes, rock gardens, raised beds, the front of borders or naturalised in grass. Soil should be free draining, but otherwise these bulbs are not fussy about their growing conditions.

GROWING METHOD

Planting Plant the bulbs in groups about 7.5cm (3in) deep and 7.5cm (3in) apart in early autumn.

Feeding A balanced granular fertiliser can be sprinkled over the soil surface in spring, but plants usually grow well without supplementary feeding, except in very poor, thin soils. Watering is necessary only in very dry conditions.

Problems Apart from occasional slug damage, plants are generally trouble free.

FLOWERING

Season Chionodoxa flowers in early spring, sometimes appearing as the snow is thawing to live up to its common name.

Cutting Flowers can be cut when they begin to open. They are valuable for cutting when few other flowers are available in the garden.

AFTER FLOWERING

Requirements Lift and divide overcrowded plants when the foliage dies down in early summer after flowering, otherwise little attention is needed.

CHIONODOXA AT A GLANCE

A low-growing bulb producing plenty of bright blue flowers in early spring.

		RECOMMENDED VARIETIES
JAN	/	
FEB	flowering	*Chionodoxa siehei:*
MAR	flowering	'Alba'
APR	flowering	'Pink Giant'
MAY	/	'Rosea'
JUN	/	
JULY	/	
AUG	/	
SEPT	plant	
OCT	/	
NOV	/	
DEC	/	

CLIVIA MINIATA
Kaffir lily

CLIVIAS MAKE SHOWY *and colourful house plants, and will bloom for many years if they are given a winter rest.*

THE PALE *creamy yellow flowers of* Clivia miniata citrina *make this unusual plant worth seeking out.*

FEATURES

This evergreen forms a striking house or conservatory plant, with long, deep green, strap-shaped leaves which overlap at the base rather like a leek. In spring or summer, a stout stem pushes between the leaf bases and grows to around 45cm (18in), carrying a head of 20 or so bright orange, bell-shaped flowers. These are marked with yellow in the throat and have prominent golden anthers.

Selected hybrids have larger flowers in various rich orange shades: a beautiful yellow-flowered variety, *C. miniata citrina*, has been developed but to date these plants are scarce and expensive, as are cultivars with cream striped foliage.

CLIVIA AT A GLANCE

A striking house plant with large heads of orange, bell-shaped flowers on stout stems. Minimum temperature 10°C.

		RECOMMENDED VARIETIES
JAN	/	
FEB	flowering	*Clivia miniata citrina*
MAR	flowering	'Striata'
APR	flowering	
MAY	transplant	
JUN	/	
JULY	/	
AUG	/	
SEPT	/	
OCT	/	
NOV	/	
DEC	/	

CONDITIONS

Aspect   Clivia prefers a reasonably bright position in the home, but not one in direct sun, which will scorch the foliage. Provide shading in a greenhouse or conservatory

Site   Grow as a room plant while it is flowering; during the summer the container can be placed in a sheltered position outdoors. Use a loam-based or soilless potting compost.

GROWING METHOD

Planting   Clivias are usually bought as house plants in growth.

Feeding   Give a high potash liquid feed every two or three weeks from early spring through the summer. Keep the compost thoroughly moist from spring to autumn, then keep the plant cool and water it very sparingly in winter.

Problems   Mealy bugs can appear as fluffy white blobs between the leaf bases; use a systemic insecticide to control them.

FLOWERING

Season   Flowers may be carried any time between late winter and early summer

Cutting   Not suitable for cutting.

AFTER FLOWERING

Requirements   Remove spent flower stalks. Repot only when essential; crowded plants tend to flower more reliably.

COLCHICUM AUTUMNALE
Autumn crocus, meadow saffron

THE DELICATE COLOUR *and form of meadow saffron flowers are particularly prominent, as they appear long before the leaves. They are very welcome as they appear in autumn when the garden is often looking rather untidy and faded after its summer exuberance.*

FEATURES

This is another lovely plant to brighten and lift the garden in autumn. It is unusual in that the 15–23cm (6–9in) high flowers emerge directly from the neck of the corm, the leaves not appearing until months later, in spring. Although the flowers look similar to crocuses, the plants are not related. Up to a dozen rose-pink to pale lilac, goblet-shaped flowers emerge from each corm. There is a pure white form, 'Alba', and a glorious double form known as 'Waterlily', which has a profusion of rose-lilac petals. Always plant in fairly large groups for the best effect.

This easy-care bulb gives great rewards. It has a long history of use in herbal medicine but all parts of the plant are poisonous.

COLCHICUM AT A GLANCE

A crocus-like plant valuable for its autumn flowers held on delicate stems.

		RECOMMENDED VARIETIES
JAN	/	
FEB	/	
MAR	/	'Alboplenum'
APR	/	'Album'
MAY	/	'Pleniflorum'
JUN	/	'The Giant'
JULY	plant	'Waterlily'
AUG	plant	
SEPT	flowering	
OCT	flowering	
NOV	flowering	
DEC	/	

CONDITIONS

Aspect   Colchicum grows in full sun or very light shade.

Site   Suitable for rock gardens, borders or for naturalising in grassed areas or in light shade under trees. For best results grow this plant in well-drained soil to which organic matter has been added.

GROWING METHOD

Planting   Corms should be planted in late summer, 7.5cm (3in) deep and 10–15cm (4–6in) apart, in groups. Established clumps are best divided at this time, too.

Feeding   Apply a generous mulch of decayed organic matter in winter. Further feeding is not usually necessary. Water in dry spells once the leaves appear in spring, and throughout their growing period.

Problems   No specific pest or disease problems are common for this plant.

FLOWERING

Season   Flowers spring out of the ground in autumn.

Cutting   Cut flowers for the vase when the goblet shape is fully formed but before it opens out. Flowers last about a week in the vase.

AFTER FLOWERING

Requirements   Spent flowers may be cut off or left on the ground. Dead foliage may need tidying up at the end of the season.

CONVALLARIA MAJALIS
Lily-of-the-valley

LONG A FAVOURITE with spring brides, fragrant lily-of-the-valley is an easy and rewarding bulb to grow.

IDEAL FOR EDGING a shady garden, these lovely plants are also completely reliable, increasing and flowering every year.

FEATURES

This is a tough little plant with a dainty appearance that belies its ease of growth. It is ideal for naturalising in shady spots in the garden and also under trees where it can grow undisturbed. The dainty little white bell flowers are borne in spring; they are delightfully scented and last well in the vase. Flower stems may be 20–25cm (8–10in) high, just topping the broadish, furled leaves which clasp the flower stems in pairs. There are several named cultivars but the straight species is by far the most popular. Previously used in folk medicine, the plant is now known to contain several poisonous substances although research continues on its potential medical use. The fleshy rhizomes with their growth shoots are known as 'pips'.

CONVALLARIA AT A GLANCE

A low-growing plant with very fragrant, dainty white bells on arching stems in late spring. Ideal for light shade.

		RECOMMENDED VARIETIES
JAN	/	
FEB	/	'Albostriata'
MAR	/	'Fortin's Giant'
APR	flowering 🌸	'Flore Pleno'
MAY	flowering 🌸	'Prolificans'
JUN	/	*Convallaria majalis rosea*
JULY	/	
AUG	/	
SEPT	/	
OCT	plant 🖐	
NOV	plant 🖐	
DEC	plant 🖐	

CONDITIONS

Aspect Prefers to grow in partial shade; ideal under deciduous trees.

Site A good ground cover plant; also suitable for mixed beds and borders. Soil should be free draining but moisture retentive, containing large amounts of decayed organic matter.

GROWING METHOD

Planting The pips are planted in late autumn about 2.5cm (1in) deep and 10cm (4in) apart. Congested clumps can be divided in autumn or winter.

Feeding In early winter apply a generous mulch of decayed manure or compost, or pile on the decaying leaves of deciduous trees. Keep soil moist throughout the growing season, giving a thorough soaking when necessary.

Problems Few problems are encountered but poor drainage may rot the root system.

FLOWERING

Season Flowers appear from mid-spring

Cutting This lovely cut flower perfumes a whole room. Pull the stems from the plant. It is traditional to use the foliage to wrap around the bunch.

AFTER FLOWERING

Requirements If possible, leave the plants undisturbed for several years. If clumps are extremely dense and flowering poor, lift and divide sections during autumn or early winter.

CRINUM
Swamp lily

LIGHT PERFUME is an added reason to grow these pretty pink crinums. They are a good choice for a sheltered border.

VERY TALL STEMS carry the white flowers of Crinum x powellii *well clear of the leaves so that the blooms are always well displayed.*

FEATURES

There are over 100 species of crinum, but *C.* x *powellii* and the more tender *C. moorei* are the two most commonly grown. Both bear large, scented, lily-like flowers in pale pink or white on stems up to 1m (3ft) high; plants have long, strap-shaped, light-green leaves. The flowers appear from middle to late summer and sometimes into autumn.

The bulbs can grow very large indeed, up to 15cm (6in) or more across, and can be very weighty. In time very large clumps are formed and they require considerable physical effort to lift and divide. Crinums need a sheltered position to do well. In cool areas they can also be grown quite successfully in containers which can be moved under cover in autumn.

CRINUM AT A GLANCE

Large, scented, lily-like flowers in late summer and autumn. This plant needs a sheltered, sunny position to thrive.

JAN	/	
FEB	/	
MAR	/	
APR	plant	
MAY	plant	
JUN	/	
JULY	/	
AUG	flowering	
SEPT	flowering	
OCT	/	
NOV	/	
DEC	/	

RECOMMENDED VARIETIES

Crinum x *powellii:*
  'Album'
  'Roseum'

Crinum moorei

Crinum bulbispermum:
  'Album'

CONDITIONS

Aspect Grow crinum in a sunny, south-facing, sheltered position. *C. moorei* is best grown in a pot in a conservatory.

Site Suitable for borders or as a specimen plant in a container on a patio or similar. Soil must be free draining but moisture retentive.

GROWING METHOD

Planting Plant in spring, which is also the best time to divide existing clumps. *C.* x *powellii* should have the neck of the bulb above soil level, while *C. moorei* should be planted with the nose of the bulb at the level of the soil.

Feeding Balanced fertiliser may be applied as new growth starts in spring. Keep the soil moist while the plants are in growth. Water plants in containers regularly.

Problems Not generally susceptible to disease or pests but snails love to eat the foliage and flowers.

FLOWERING

Season Flowers appear during summer and into the autumn months.

Cutting It is possible to cut blooms for the house but they last longer on the plant.

AFTER FLOWERING

Requirements Cut off the flowering stalk once the flowers are over. Protect the crowns with a mulch of peat over winter, or move plants under cover. Disturb established plants as little as possible.

CROCOSMIA
Montbretia

THE VIBRANT COLOUR of crocosmia flowers gives great decorative value but is matched by vigorous growth that may need to be controlled.

THE CLEAR, GOLDEN YELLOW flowers of 'Citronella' make a pleasant change from the intense orange-reds of other varieties.

FEATURES

Also known as montbretia, some types of crocosmia are extremely vigorous and can become invasive in warm areas. It will often survive in old, neglected gardens where virtually everything else has disappeared. The foliage is slender, sword-shaped, and upright or slightly arching. The flowers are carried on double-sided spikes which also arch gracefully, reaching some 60–90cm (2–3ft) tall. Most types have eye-catching bright reddish-orange flowers which open progressively from the base of the spike. In cold areas, plants should be protected with a mulch of dry leaves over winter, and should be planted in a reasonably sheltered position.

CROCOSMIA AT A GLANCE

A vigorous plant with sword-shaped leaves and brightly coloured spikes of flowers through the summer.

		RECOMMENDED VARIETIES
JAN	/	
FEB	/	'Bressingham Blaze'
MAR	plant	'Canary Bird'
APR	plant	'Citronella'
MAY	/	'Emily McKenzie'
JUN	/	'Jackanapes'
JULY	flowering	'Lucifer'
AUG	flowering	'Solfaterre'
SEPT	flowering	
OCT	/	
NOV	/	
DEC	/	

CONDITIONS

Aspect	Grows best in a fully open, sunny position.
Site	Good in beds or borders in well-drained soil.

GROWING METHOD

Planting	Plant corms in spring, 7.5cm (3in) deep and about 15cm (6in) apart. Pot-grown specimens can be planted throughout the spring and summer, even when in flower. It usually becomes necessary to thin out clumps every few years.
Feeding	A balanced fertiliser can be applied in early summer, but feeding is not generally necessary.
Problems	There are no pests or diseases that commonly attack crocosmia.

FLOWERING

Season	There is a long flowering period all through summer. Congested clumps often seem to produce more blooms.
Cutting	Flowers are not suitable for cutting and are better appreciated in the garden.

AFTER FLOWERING

Requirements	Cut off spent flower stems as soon as the blooms have faded to avoid seed setting and plants spreading. Once the leaves have died down, protect the corms with a mulch of straw or dry leaves in all but very warm, sheltered gardens.

CROCUS
Crocus

SAFFRON CROCUS (*Crocus sativus*) *displays branched bright orange stigmas, the source of saffron, the costly spice used in cooking.*

CROCUS CHRYSANTHUS 'ARD SCHENK' – *one of the most popular species – pushes up white goblet-shaped flowers in spring*

FEATURES

There are over 80 species of crocus, mainly late winter and spring flowering, but there are some autumn bloomers, too. Crocus are among the earliest flowers to appear in spring, often pushing their flowers up through the snow. In some species flowers appear some weeks before the leaves. Crocus are mostly native to the countries around the Mediterranean Sea where they usually grow at high altitudes. They do, however, extend as far east as Afghanistan.

Appearance Crocus foliage is short, rather sparse and looks like a broad-leaf grass. The lovely little goblet-shaped flowers are borne on short stems 6–12cm (2–5in) high. Most are blue, violet, white, yellow or cream but some species have pink flowers. Many have deeper coloured stripes or feathering on the petals.

Uses Although unsuitable for cutting, these little bulbous plants are one of the greatest delights of the garden. They are often mass planted in garden beds, especially at the front of borders. They can be naturalised in lawns or grouped together under deciduous trees. Crocuses are excellent plants for rock gardens and they make good container plants, being especially suitable for winter and early spring window-boxes. The floral display of some individual species in the garden can be short, but by growing a selection of species you can enjoy these charming flowers over an extended period, from early autumn virtually right through to late spring.

POPULAR SPECIES

Spring Some of the most popular spring-flowering species are *C. biflorus*, *C. chrysanthus*, *C. flavus*, *C. minimus*, *C. tommasinianus* and *C. vernus*. Cultivars of a number of these species are available, with the many and varied cultivars of *C. chrysanthus* being especially popular, although each of these species have their admirers. *C. ancyrensis* is particularly early flowering, appearing in January and February.

Autumn Autumn-flowering species include *C. kotschyanus*, *C. niveus*, *C. laevigatus*, *C. longiflorus*, *C. nudiflorus*, *C. sativus* (the saffron crocus), *C. serotinus* (also known as *C. salzmannii*) and *C. speciosus*. *Crocus sativus* is well known as the source of the costliest of all herbs and spices. Native to temperate Eurasia and widely grown in Mediterranean regions, saffron crocus needs a very specific climate to flourish and is an extremely labour-intensive crop to harvest. Saffron comes only from the stigmas of the flowers and 154,000 flowers are needed to make up a kilogram of pure saffron.

CONDITIONS

Aspect Prefers an open, sunny position but may be grown in light shade.

Site Good for rock gardens, raised beds, the fronts of borders or naturalised in grass. Soil must be well drained, preferably containing plenty of well-rotted organic matter.

THESE CYCLAMEN COUM *are thriving in an alpine-type sink garden: when they are allowed to self-seed, they soon form dense colonies. The marbled leaves are attractive, as well as the dainty, pale pink and purple flowers with their upswept petals.*

CONDITIONS

Aspect   The ideal situation for hardy cyclamen is beneath deciduous trees where there is some winter sun but dappled sunlight for the rest of the year. In the home, florists' cyclamen need a cool, bright position.

Site   Hardy cyclamen can be grown on rock gardens, under trees and shrubs, and in borders. The soil must be well drained with a high organic content. Indoors, choose a bright, cool windowsill or a conservatory.

GROWING METHOD

Planting   The flattened tubers (often wrongly referred to as corms) should be planted with their tops just below the soil surface. Plant in late summer and early autumn at about 15cm (6in) intervals. Pot-grown seedlings are easier to establish than dry tubers, and can be obtained from garden centres and specialist nurseries.

Feeding   If soil is poor, a sprinkling of balanced fertiliser can be given when growth begins and again after flowering. Florists' cyclamen should be given high potash liquid fertiliser every 14 days from when the flower buds appear until flowering is over. Water carefully from the base to avoid splashing the top of the tuber; never leave the pots standing in water.

Problems   Florists' cyclamen grown indoors often succumb to overwatering, drying out, and a dry, overwarm atmosphere. Vine weevils are attracted to the tubers and may cause the sudden collapse of the plant: use a soil insecticide if they are caught in time.

CYCLAMEN AT A GLANCE

Characteristic, upswept petals on a mound-forming plant with attractive marbled foliage. Suitable for outdoors or as pot plants.

		RECOMMENDED VARIETIES
JAN	flowering	*Cyclamen cilicium album*
FEB	flowering	*Cyclamen coum album*
MAR	flowering	*Cyclamen hederifolium*
APR	flowering	'Bowles' Apollo'
MAY	/	'Silver Cloud'
JUN	/	*Cyclamen libanoticum*
JULY	plant	*Cyclamen pseudibericum*
AUG	plant	*Cyclamen purpurascens*
SEPT	flowering	*Cyclamen repandum*
OCT	flowering	*Cyclamen persicum:* many
NOV	flowering	hybrids available
DEC	flowering	

FLOWERING

Season   *C. persicum* flowers through winter into spring. *C. hederifolium* has a long flowering period in autumn, while *C. coum* and *C. repandum* flower betwen late winter and spring.

Cutting   Pull flowers from the plant with a rolling motion and cut off the thin base of the stalk.

AFTER FLOWERING

Requirements   Outdoors, leave spent flowering stems to set seed and do not disturb tubers. After flowering, allow pot plants to die down and keep dry over summer. Start into growth again in August.

CYRTANTHUS ELATUS
Vallota, Scarborough lily

'PAGODA' I
hybrids, with

FEAT

FE/

green lea

TH
Da

Pro

SCARLET FLOWERS *with a flared, trumpet-like shape make Scarborough lily a most striking plant.*

IN WARM AREAS *Scarborough lily can be grown outdoors, but it is more reliable as a pot plant for the conservatory or greenhouse.*

FEATURES

Still more commonly known under its earlier botanical name of *Vallota*, this old favourite should be more widely grown. Four or more brilliant scarlet, open trumpet-shaped blooms are held on a sturdy stem some 45cm (18in) tall among dark green, strappy leaves. The plant originates from South Africa, and unfortunately, is not hardy enough to try outdoors except in the most favoured, warmest areas of the country. However, it makes a good pot plant for a cool greenhouse or conservatory, or it can be grown indoors on a sunny windowsill. During the summer, the pots can be taken outside to decorate the patio. The Scarborough lily is not difficult to cultivate, and deserves to be more popular.

CONDITIONS

Aspect   Grows best in a bright, sunny position.
Site   Must be grown as a house or greenhouse plant
             in all but the very warmest areas of the
             country.

GROWING METHOD

Planting   Plant bulbs in summer with the tip of the
               bulb just at or above soil level. Set one bulb in
               a 12.5cm (5in) pot.
Feeding   Apply liquid fertiliser every 14 days as soon as
               growth appears. Keep the plant well watered
               throughout the spring and summer, but
               reduce watering after flowering.
Problems   No specific pest or disease problems are known
               for this plant.

FLOWERING

Season   Flowers usually appear in mid-summer.
Cutting Flowers will last well when cut but probably
             give better decorative value if they are left on
             the plant.

AFTER FLOWERING

Requirements Cut off the spent flower stems. Reduce
                 watering and allow the compost to dry out
                 completely between late winter and mid-
                 spring. Do not repot for several years as the
                 plants flower best when the pot is crowded.
                 Offsets are produced freely, and some of these
                 may be removed to pot up and grow on to
                 flowering size in two or three years.

CYRTANTHUS AT A GLANCE

A tender bulb with large, trumpet-shaped flowers in summer – an excellent house or greenhouse plant. Min 7°C (45°F)

		RECOMMENDED VARIETIES
JAN	/	'Pink Diamond
FEB	/	
MAR	/	
APR	/	
MAY	/	
JUN	plant	
JULY	flowering	
AUG	flowering	
SEPT	flowering	
OCT	/	
NOV	/	
DEC	/	

EUCOMIS COMOSA
Pineapple lily

SILKY
stems of

THE STAT
make this bo

FE

FEAT

THE TUFT on top of the flower spike does resemble a pineapple, but the pretty individual flowers below give a softer impression.

THE ROBUST GROWTH of this clump of pineapple lilies shows that the growing conditions in this spot are ideal.

FEATURES

This South African plant gets its common name from the pineapple-like flower spike with its topknot of tufted leaves. The greenish-white or white flowers, sometimes tinged with pink, are scented and packed tightly on to the spike; their weight can sometimes cause the stem to flop over. The broad, sword-shaped leaves are light green and attractively spotted with purple on the underside. This flower is always of interest, whether in the garden or as a potted plant: blooms are extremely long lasting when cut. Another species in cultivation is *E. bicolor,* with attractive green and purple flowers. Both species grow to about 60cm (24in). Pineapple lily grows from a fleshy bulbous rootstock and is dormant in winter.

CONDITIONS

Aspect Prefers full sun but tolerates light shade. Grows best in warm, sheltered areas, but can also be grown in colder gardens if the rootstock is protected or lifted for winter.

Site Eucomis is good for the middle or back of the flower border. Needs well-drained soil enriched with decayed organic matter before planting time.

GROWING METHOD

Planting Plant in spring, 5–10cm (2–4in) deep and 20–30cm (8–12in) apart.

Feeding Apply complete plant food as new growth begins. Mulch around plants in summer with well-decayed compost or manure. Keep the soil moist while the plant is actively growing.

Problems No specific problems are known.

FLOWERING

Season Flowers during mid-summer.

Cutting The pineapple lily is usually enjoyed as a specimen garden plant, but if there are enough blooms, or if the stems are broken by wind, the cut flowers may last for several weeks if the vase water is changed regularly.

AFTER FLOWERING

Requirements Cut down the flowering stem once the flowers have passed their best. Either dig up the bulb and overwinter in a frost-free place, or in mild districts, mulch the planting area with peat or dry leaves to protect the bulb over winter.

EUCOMIS AT A GLANCE		
A tall, striking bulb with a pineapple-like flower stem. A sunny, sheltered spot is required.		
JAN	/	
FEB	/	
MAR	plant	RECOMMENDED VARIETIES
APR	plant	
MAY	/	*Eucomis bicolor*
JUN	/	*E. b.* 'Alba'
JULY	flowering	*E. comosa*
AUG	flowering	*E. pole-evansii*
SEPT	/	*E. zambesiaca*
OCT	/	
NOV	/	
DEC	/	

A per
pink l

JAN	
FEB	
MA	
AP	
MA	
JU	
JU	
AU	
SEF	
OC	
NC	
DE	

Tall, statel
masses of i

JAN	/
FEB	
MAR	
APR	
MAY	/
JUN	f
JULY	f
AUG	/
SEPT	F
OCT	F
NOV	/
DEC	

C

As

Sit

FREESIA
Freesia species and hybrids

THE SPECIES Freesia alba (also known as F. refracta) is the most heavily scented of all freesias, but can be difficult to find.

THERE ARE MANY hybrid varieties of freesia, some with strikingly bicoloured flowers like these. Most, but not all, are sweetly scented.

FEATURES

Freesias are loved for their strong perfume as well as their appearance. The wild species have yellow or white flowers and may grow about 30cm (12in) high: modern hybrids grow 45cm (18in) or more high and are available in a wide range of colours which includes blue, mauve, pink, red and purple. However, some of these large-flowered hybrids have no scent. The white-flowered *F. alba* (*F. refracta*) is generally considered to have the best perfume.

For growing outdoors, buy specially prepared freesias and plant them in a sheltered position; they will flower in summer. Other freesias should be planted in containers which are brought into the house and greenhouse in autumn for winter flowering.

FREESIA AT A GLANCE

Fragrant, tubular flowers in a wide range of colours are held on delicate spikes. Grow indoors or outside in a sheltered position.

JAN flowering** 🌱		RECOMMENDED VARIETIES
FEB flowering** 🌱		
MAR flowering** 🌱		'Diana'
APR plant 🌱*		'Fantasy'
MAY /		'Oberon'
JUN /		'Romany'
JULY plant 🌱**		'White Swan'
AUG plant 🌱**/flowering 🌱*		'Yellow River'
SEPT flowering* 🌱		
OCT flowering* 🌱		
NOV /		
DEC /		

** indoors   *outdoors

CONDITIONS

Aspect — Freesias prefer full sun but tolerate very light shade for part of the day.

Site Grow outdoors in a sheltered border. For winter flowers, plant in pots in summer, standing the pots in a sheltered position outside until autumn, then bring them into a cool greenhouse or conservatory to flower. Use free-draining, John Innes or soilless potting compost.

GROWING METHOD

Planting Outdoors, plant 5cm (2in) deep and the same distance apart in mid-spring. For pot culture, plant 5cm (2in) deep, six to a 12.5cm (5in) pot in July.

Feeding Apply a high potash liquid fertiliser every 14 days through the growing season. Keep the compost just moist at all times.

Problems Aphids may attack the flower stems. Control with a contact insecticide when necessary.

FLOWERING

Season From middle to late winter through to mid-spring indoors, late summer outside.

Cutting Cut when the lowest flower on the spike is fully open and other buds are well developed.

AFTER FLOWERING

Requirements Remove spent flower stems. When the foliage dies down, lift corms and store them in dry peat until it is time for replanting.

FRITILLARIA
Crown imperial, snake's head fritillary

THE FLOWERS of snake's head fritillary bear a distinctive, intricately checkered pattern that looks a bit like a game board.

SNAKE'S HEAD FRITILLARY is probably the easiest fritillary to grow and is ideal for damp meadows or woodlands.

FEATURES

The name fritillary comes from the Latin word *fritillus*, meaning 'dice-box', as the checkered patterns on the flowers of some of the species resemble the checkerboards associated with many games played with dice. There are about 100 species of this striking bulbous plant, which is related to the lilies, but only a relatively small number are in general cultivation. The form and colour of the flowers varies considerably from one species to another, and some are fascinating rather than beautiful. The flowers are generally pendent and bell shaped, carried on leafy stems; their height varies considerably, from low-growing rock garden plants such as the 10–15cm (4–6in) *Fritillaria michailovskyi*, to the stately and imposing crown imperials (*F. imperialis*), which can reach well over 1m (3ft) tall. Many fritillaries, especially crown imperial, have a strong 'foxy' scent to them which some people find unpleasant. All parts of the plant, including the bulbs, possess this scent, which can be quite penetrating.

Uses These plants, especially crown imperial, deserve a prominent place in the spring garden. They are sometimes seen taking pride of place in a bulb garden but are more often included in a mixed border planting with other bulbs and perennials. To show them to their best advantage, plant several of the same type together as individual plants will not have the same impact. Those that multiply readily, such as the snake's head fritillary, can be naturalised in dappled shade. All species can be grown in containers but most are easier to grow in the open ground.

Availability Crown imperials and snake's head fritillaries are readily available from garden centres, but some of the other species may have to be obtained from mail order bulb specialists.

TYPES

F. imperialis The best known fritillary is the majestic crown imperial, *F. imperialis*, which has a cluster of orange, yellow or red bell-shaped flowers hanging below a crown of green leaves on a stem 50–100cm (20–39in) high.

F. meleagris The snake's head fritillary or checkered lily, *F. meleagris*, occurs in the wild in meadows throughout Europe and is one of the easiest to cultivate. The checkered flowers occur in shades of green, purple, magenta or white.

Others Among the many other species worth growing are *F. acmopetala*, with bell-shaped green and brown flowers; *F. biflora* 'Martha Roderick', with brown-streaked cream flowers, *F. camschatcensis*, with very deep purple, almost black flowers; *F. michailovskyi*, with yellow-tipped purple bells, *F. pallidiflora*, with soft yellow flowers veined lime-green or burgundy; *F. persica* with deep purple flowers; *F. pontica* with greenish bells; and *F. pyrenaica*, a deep burgundy purple, spotted green outside while the inside is purple-checked green.

CROWN IMPERIAL (Fritillaria imperialis) is an exciting fritillary that takes pride of place in many keen bulb growers' gardens. The 'crown' referred to in the common name is the topknot of leaves from which the bell-shaped flowers are suspended.

CONDITIONS

Aspect Fritillary grows best in light shade or with morning sun and afternoon shade. Some species take full sun. All are best with protection from strong wind.

Site Fritillaries can be grown in beds and borders, on rockeries, or in containers, according to species. *F. meleagris* can be naturalised in grass. Soil for fritillaries must be well drained but should contain plenty of well-rotted compost or manure. The area around the plants should be well mulched, too. *F. meleagris* prefers a more moisture-retentive soil than some of the other species.

FRITILLARIA AT A GLANCE

Unusual bulbs in a wide range of sizes and flower forms, with striking, pendent, bell-shaped blooms.

JAN	/	
FEB	/	
MAR	/	
APR	flowering	🌸
MAY	flowering	🌸
JUN	/	
JULY	/	
AUG	/	
SEPT	plant	🌿
OCT	plant	🌿
NOV	plant	🌿
DEC	/	

RECOMMENDED VARIETIES

Fritillaria biflora:
 'Martha Roderick'

Fritillaria imperialis:
 'Lutea'
 'Rubra Maxima'
 'Prolifera
 'The Premier'

Fritillaria persica:
 'Adiyaman'

GROWING METHOD

Planting The lily-like bulbs can dry out quickly and should be planted as soon as they are available. Planting depth varies between 5–20cm (2–8in) depending on species. Plant the large bulbs of crown imperials on their sides on a layer of sand so that water does not collect in the hollow centre.

Feeding Apply a general fertiliser after flowering or a high potash fertiliser in early spring as growth starts. Water in dry spells during the growing season, especially before flowering.

Problems Bulbs may rot in badly drained soil.

FLOWERING

Season Flowers appear from mid-spring to early summer.

Cutting Despite being fairly long-lasting as a cut flower, blooms are rarely used this way because of the unpleasant smell of some flowers. Unfortunately crown imperial is one of these. However, they are so striking in the garden that they are best enjoyed there.

AFTER FLOWERING

Requirements Once flowers have faded, flowering stems can be cut down, but leave the flowerheads on snake's head fritillaries to set seed. Bulbs are best left undisturbed, but if necessary clumps can be divided in summer and replanted immediately.

GALANTHUS
Snowdrop

TRUE HARBINGERS of spring, snowdrops are among the first bulbs to appear in late winter, often pushing up through the snow.

THE DOUBLE SNOWDROP, Galanthus nivalis 'Flore Pleno', is an easily grown, vigorous and reliable variety.

FEATURES

The snowdrop (*G. nivalis*) is well loved for flowering in late winter while conditions are still very bleak. Most of the dozen or so species flower in late winter to early spring although there is one autumn-flowering species (*G. reginae-olgae*). *G. elwesii* and *G. caucasicus* are also very early bloomers. There are named varieties of several species available. *G. nivalis* grows only 10–12.5cm (4–5in) high, but taller varieties such as *G. elwesii* can grow up to 25cm (10in). The nodding flowers have three long, pure white petals and three shorter ones marked with a bright green horseshoe shape. The dark green foliage may be matt or glossy but is normally shorter than the flowers.

GALANTHUS AT A GLANCE

A small, dainty bulb popular for its late winter and early spring flowers. Very hardy.

	RECOMMENDED VARIETIES
JAN flowering	'Atkinsii'
FEB flowering	'Cordelia'
MAR flowering / plant 'in the green'	'Sam Arnott'
APR /	*Galanthus lutescens:*
MAY /	'Magnet'
JUN /	*Galanthus nivalis:*
JULY /	'Flore Pleno'
AUG /	'Lady Elphinstone'
SEPT plant	'Lutescens'
OCT plant	'Pusey Green Tip'
NOV /	'Scharlockii'
DEC flowering	'Viridapicis'

CONDITIONS

Aspect Grows best in shade or dappled sunlight.
Site Ideal for rockeries, the fronts of beds and borders or naturalising under deciduous trees. Soil must contain plenty of decayed organic matter to prevent excessive drying out in summer. Mulching in autumn with old manure, compost or leafmould is beneficial.

GROWING METHOD

Planting Plant bulbs in autumn 8–10cm (3–4in) deep (deeper in light soils) and about the same apart. Do not allow the bulbs to dry out before planting. Snowdrops are much more reliable when transplanted while in growth, after flowering – known as planting 'in the green'. Plants are available from specialist suppliers in late winter or early spring.
Feeding Mulch during autumn with decayed organic matter. Watering is not usually necessary.
Problems No specific problems are known.

FLOWERING

Season Flowering is from winter through to spring, depending on species.
Cutting Flowers can be cut for indoor decoration.

AFTER FLOWERING

Requirements Existing clumps can be lifted, divided and replanted as soon as the flowers have faded. Do not leave the plants out of the soil any longer than necessary.

GLADIOLUS CALLIANTHUS
Acidanthera

EACH BLOOM carries an attractive central, deep purple blotch, and has a slightly uneven, star-like shape.

THE SWEETLY-SCENTED white blooms of acidanthera appear late in the summer, when many other bulbs are over.

FEATURES

Although this plant is now classified as a species of gladiolus, many gardeners still know it better under its previous botanical name of *Acidanthera murielae*. The pure white, slightly drooping blooms have a dark purple central blotch, and are sweetly scented; their similarity to a gladiolus flower is obvious, but they are more delicate and graceful. The leaves are erect and sword shaped, growing to about 60cm (2ft). The flowers – up to a dozen per corm – are held on slender stems above the tips of the leaves, and appear in late summer.
This is not a plant for cold, exposed gardens, requiring a warm, sunny position to do well. In cold regions it can be grown successfully as a conservatory or cool greenhouse plant.

G. CALLIANTHUS AT A GLANCE

A late summer flowering plant with attractive, white, scented blooms. Suitable for growing outdoors in mild areas only.

		RECOMMENDED VARIETIES
JAN	/	'Murieliae'
FEB	/	
MAR	plant (indoors)	
APR	plant (outdoors)	
MAY	/	
JUN	/	
JULY	/	
AUG	flowering	
SEPT	flowering	
OCT	/	
NOV	/	
DEC	/	

CONDITIONS

Aspect These plants require full sun.
Site Acidantheras can be grown in a sheltered, sunny spot outside in mild areas: otherwise grow the corms in pots in a greenhouse or conservatory, moving the pots on to a sheltered patio or similar position in midsummer. Light, free-draining soil is required. In pots, use soilless or John Innes potting compost.

GROWING METHOD

Planting Plant in late spring, 10cm (4in) deep and 20–25cm (8–10in) apart.
Feeding Give an occasional application of high potash liquid fertiliser (such as rose or tomato feed) during the growing season. Pot-grown plants should be fed every 10–14 days. Watering is not necessary for plants in the open ground except in very dry conditions; water pot-grown plants sufficiently to keep the compost just moist.
Problems Plants may fail to flower in cold, exposed gardens. Corms may rot in heavy, clay soils.

FLOWERING

Season Flowers in late summer – mid August through September.
Cutting Pick the stems when the buds are showing white at their tips.

AFTER FLOWERING

Requirements Allow the foliage to die down, then lift the corms before the first frosts. Allow them to dry, brush off soil and store in dry, cool, frost-free conditions until the following spring.

GLORIOSA
Glory lily

FLUTED RECURVED PETALS give these flowers an airy, floating effect. Plants grow rapidly in warm, humid conditions.

THESE GLORIOSA LILIES at various stages of development display a fascinating range of colours and shapes.

FEATURES

This climber is always sure to attract attention. It grows from elongated, finger-like tubers, and needs greenhouse or conservatory conditions. A plant will grow up to 2.4m (8ft) in the right conditions, its long, slender stems twining their way through netting or wooden trellis supports by means of tendrils at the tips of the lance-shaped leaves. The unusual lily-like flowers are crimson and yellow, with their wavy-edged petals strongly recurved to show the prominent, curving stamens.

Gloriosa has a long flowering period through summer and autumn and usually gives a spectacular display. It is worth growing in a prominent position where it can be admired, but it is not hardy enough to grow outdoors.

GLORIOSA AT A GLANCE

A greenhouse climber with spectacular summer flowers. Minimum temperature 10°C (50°F).

		RECOMMENDED VARIETIES
JAN	plant	
FEB	plant	*Gloriosa superba:*
MAR	plant	'Rothschildiana'
APR	/	'Lutea'
MAY	/	
JUN	/	
JULY	flowering	
AUG	flowering	
SEPT	flowering	
OCT	/	
NOV	/	
DEC	/	

CONDITIONS

Aspect Grow in a greenhouse or conservatory, in bright light but shaded from direct summer sun.

Site Use either soilless or John Innes potting compost.

GROWING METHOD

Planting The tubers are planted out in late winter or early spring about 5cm (2in) deep, placing one tuber in a 15cm (6in) pot of moist compost. Take care not to injure the tips of the tubers.

Feeding Apply high potash liquid fertiliser every 14 days during the growing season. Water sparingly until growth commences, more freely during active growth but never allow the soil to become waterlogged.

Problems Slugs may attack the tubers, and poor drainage or overwatering will rot them.

FLOWERING

Season Flowers throughout the summer.

Cutting Flowers last well when picked.

AFTER FLOWERING

Requirements Snap off flowers as they fade. Reduce watering when flowering has finished and allow the tubers to dry out for the winter. Store them dry in their pots or in dry peat in a minimum temperature of 10°C (50°F) and replant in spring.

HEDYCHIUM
Ginger lily

LONG RED STAMENS contrast nicely with the clear yellow flowers on this kahili ginger. The flowers have a strong perfume.

THIS GINGER LILY needs room to spread out and show off its strong lines. It is a useful landscaping plant.

FEATURES

There are over 40 species of ginger lily although not many species are in cultivation. These plants are strong growers, mostly to about 1.8m (6ft), their growth originating from sturdy rhizomes. They can be bedded out in borders for the summer, or grown in tubs as a patio or greenhouse and conservatory plant. Mid-green leaves are lance shaped.

The tall, showy heads of flowers are carried in late summer. White ginger or garland flower, *H. coronarium*, has white and yellow, very fragrant flowers while scarlet or red ginger lily, *H. coccineum*, has faintly scented but most attractive blooms in various shades of red, pink or salmon. Also heavily scented is kahili ginger, *H. gardnerianum*, with large, clear yellow flowers and prominent red stamens.

HEDYCHIUM AT A GLANCE

Large, showy leaves are topped by striking heads of many flowers, often scented. Needs a minimum temperature of 7°C (45°F).

JAN	/	**RECOMMENDED VARIETIES**	
FEB	/		
MAR	plant	*Hedychium coccineum*	
		aurantiacum	
APR	plant	*Hedychium coccineum:*	
MAY	/	'Tara'	
JUN	/	*H. coronarium*	
JULY	flowering	*H. densiflorum:*	
AUG	flowering	'Assam Orange'	
SEPT	flowering	*H. gardnerianum*	
OCT	/		
NOV	/		
DEC	/		

CONDITIONS

Aspect Needs a bright, sunny spot.
Site In cold areas, grow in a greenhouse or conservatory; otherwise grow in a sheltered border outside. Rich, moisture-retentive soil is necessary; add well-rotted organic matter before planting time.

GROWING METHOD

Planting Plant in spring, with the tip of the rhizome just buried below the soil surface. Space rhizomes about 60cm (24in) apart.
Feeding A balanced fertiliser can be applied as growth begins in spring. Keep the soil moist throughout the growing season.
Problems There are generally no particular problems experienced.

FLOWERING

Season Flowers in mid to late summer and early autumn.
Cutting Flowers can be cut for indoor decoration but they will last very much longer on the plant.

AFTER FLOWERING

Requirements Cut flower stems down to the ground once the flowers have faded. Lift the rhizomes when the foliage has died down and overwinter in dry peat in a frost-free place, replanting the following spring. Pot plants can be left in their pots over winter. Rhizomes may be divided in spring to increase your stock.

HIPPEASTRUM

Hippeastrum, amaryllis

'APPLE BLOSSOM' is a cultivar with unusual soft, pastel flowers. Most hippeastrums have very strongly coloured flowers in the red range.

BIG, SHOWY TRUMPET FLOWERS on stout stems are a hallmark of hippeastrums.

FEATURES

There are many species of hippeastrum but the most familiar plants, with their very large, trumpet-shaped flowers, are cultivars or hybrids of a number of species. They are popular winter-flowering house plants; between two and six large flowers are carried on thick stems that are generally over 50cm (20in) high. Blooms appear all the more spectacular because they appear ahead of the leaves or just as the leaves are emerging. There are many cultivars available but most flowers are in various shades of red, pink or white, separately or in combination. Because of the very large size of the bulb it is normal to use only one bulb per 18cm (7in) pot. The bulbs should be allowed to rest during summer if they are to be brought into bloom again.

HIPPEASTRUM AT A GLANCE

A windowsill plant with very showy, large, trumpet-shaped flowers on tall stems in winter and spring. Minimum 13°C.

		Recommended Varieties
Jan	flowering	'Apple Blossom'
Feb	flowering	'Bouquet'
Mar	flowering	'Lady Jane'
Apr	flowering	'Lucky Strike'
May	/	'Mont Blanc'
Jun	/	'Flower Record'
July	/	'Oscar'
Aug	/	'Picotee'
Sept	/	'Star of Holland'
Oct	plant	
Nov	plant	
Dec	plant	

CONDITIONS

Aspect Needs full sun and bright conditions.

Site Grow as a pot plant in the home or greenhouse. Use soilless potting compost.

GROWING METHOD

Planting Plant with about half to one-third of the bulb above soil level in a pot just large enough to hold the bulb comfortably. Bulbs can be planted any time between October and March. Use 'prepared' bulbs for Christmas and early winter flowers.

Feeding Apply a high potash liquid feed every 10–14 days once the bulb starts into growth. Water sparingly until the bud appears, then more freely until the foliage begins to die down.

Problems No problems usually, but overwatering can cause the bulb to rot.

FLOWERING

Season Showy flowers appear in about eight weeks after planting, between late December and late spring.

Cutting With frequent water changes flowers can last well, but are usually best left on the plant.

AFTER FLOWERING

Requirements Remove spent flower stems, continue to water and feed until foliage starts to yellow and die down. Allow the bulbs to dry off in a cool place, repot in fresh compost and resume watering in autumn to start them into growth.

HYACINTHOIDES
Bluebell

AN ALL-TIME FAVOURITE, *clear sky-blue bluebells don't need a lot of attention to produce a lovely display year after year.*

NATURALISED UNDER TREES, *these Spanish bluebells revel in the moist soil formed from the decaying leaf litter.*

FEATURES

This is the ideal bulb for naturalising under deciduous trees or for planting in large drifts in the garden. The delicately scented blue flowers are a great foil for many spring-flowering shrubs which have pink or white flowers: there is a white and a pink form but the blue is undoubtedly the most popular. The botanical names of these plants have undergone several changes in recent years, and they are sometimes listed under endymion and scilla as well as hyacinthoides. The Spanish bluebell (*H. hispanica*) is a little larger, up to 30cm (12in) high, and more upright in growth than the English bluebell (*H. non-scripta*). Bluebells multiply rapidly and can be very invasive. They can also be grown in containers.

HYACINTHOIDES AT A GLANCE

Well-known and loved blue flowers in mid to late spring, ideal for naturalising under deciduous trees.

		RECOMMENDED VARIETIES
JAN	/	
FEB	/	*Hyacinthoides hispanica:*
MAR	/	'Danube'
APR	flowering 🌿	'Queen of the Pinks'
MAY	flowering 🌿	'White City'
JUN	/	
JULY	/	*Hyacinthoides non-scripta:*
AUG	plant ✍	'Pink Form'
SEPT	plant ✍	'White Form'
OCT	plant ✍	
NOV	/	
DEC	/	

CONDITIONS

Aspect   These woodland plants prefer dappled sunlight or places where they receive some morning sun with shade later in the day.

Site   Perfect when naturalised under deciduous trees; bluebells also grow well in borders but don't let them smother delicate plants. A moisture-retentive soil with plenty of organic matter suits them best.

GROWING METHOD

Planting   Plant bulbs 5cm (2in) deep and about 8–10cm (3–4in) apart in late summer or early autumn. The white bulbs are fleshy and brittle; take care not to damage them when planting.

Feeding   Not normally required.

Problems   No specific problems are usually experienced.

FLOWERING

Season   Flowers from middle to late spring, with a long display in cool seasons. Flowers do not last as well if sudden high spring temperatures are experienced.

Cutting   Not suitable for cutting.

AFTER FLOWERING

Requirements   Remove spent flower stems unless you require plants to seed themselves. Keep the soil moist until the foliage dies down. The bulbs are best left undisturbed, but overcrowded clumps can be lifted and divided in late summer and replanted immediately.

HYACINTHUS ORIENTALIS

Hyacinth

WELL-ROUNDED FLOWER SPIKES are characteristic of the fine hyacinth cultivars available today. They make excellent pot plants.

HYACINTHS, with cool white flowers and dark green foliage, combine with a silvery groundcover to make a pretty garden picture.

FEATURES

Sweet-scented hyacinths are favourites in the garden or as potted plants. In the garden they look their best mass planted in blocks of one colour. They are widely grown commercially both for cut flowers and as potted flowering plants. Flower stems may be from 15–30cm (6–12in) high and the colour range includes various shades of blue, pink and rose, plus white, cream and yellow. Individual flowers are densely crowded onto the stem, making a solid-looking flowerhead. Bulbs usually flower best in their first year, the second and subsequent years producing fewer, looser blooms. Some people with sensitive skin can get a reaction from handling hyacinth bulbs, so wear gloves if you think you may be affected.

Types
The most popular hyacinths are the so-called Dutch hybrids; many varieties are available from garden centres and mail order bulb suppliers. Blues range from deep violet to pale china blue: the rose range includes deep rosy red, salmon and light pink. As well as white varieties, there are those with cream and clear yellow flowers. Some varieties have flowers with a lighter eye or a deeper coloured stripe on the petals, giving a two-tone effect. Roman hyacinths – *H. orientalis albulus* – have smaller flowers loosely arranged on the stems: Multiflora varieties have been treated so that they produce several loosely packed flower spikes from each bulb, and have a delicate appearance which makes them ideal for growing in pots. Cynthella hyacinths are miniatures growing to about 15cm (6in), usually sold in colour mixtures.

CONDITIONS

Aspect
Does well in sun or partial shade but does not like heavy shade.

Site
Grow hyacinths in pots and bowls indoors; pots and tubs outside and in flower borders. Soil must be well drained.

GROWING METHOD

Planting
Plant bulbs 15cm (6in) deep and 20cm (8in) apart in early to mid-autumn. Apply compost or rotted manure as a mulch after planting.

Feeding
Apply a balanced general fertiliser after flowering. Watering is not usually necessary in beds and borders, but bulbs in containers must be kept just moist during the growing season.

Problems
Hyacinths are not generally susceptible to pest and disease problems, though bulbs will rot if soil conditions are too wet. Forced bulbs indoors often fail to flower if they have not had the correct cold, dark period after planting.

FLOWERING

Season
Flowers appear from late winter to mid-spring. 'Prepared' bulbs should be used for Christmas flowering, and must be planted in September.

Cutting
Blooms may be cut for the vase where they will last about a week if the water is changed daily.

AFTER FLOWERING

Requirements
Remove spent flower stems and continue to water and feed the plants until the foliage starts to yellow and die down.

BLUE AND WHITE are always an effective combination, a proposition amply demonstrated by this formal garden in which deep violet-blue hyacinths stud a bed of white pansies. Although they are often grown in pots, hyacinths are at their most beautiful in a setting such as this.

POTTED HYACINTHS

Features
Potted hyacinths in bloom make a lovely cut flower substitute and are ideal as gifts. They can be grown to flower in midwinter when their colour and fragrance are most welcome.

Outdoors
If growing hyacinths outdoors choose a container at least 15cm (6in) deep so that you can place a layer of potting compost in the base of the pot before planting. Bury the bulbs 10cm (4in) below the surface of the compost. Water to moisten the compost thoroughly after planting and place the pot where it will receive sun for at least half a day. Don't water again until the compost is feeling dry or until the shoots appear. When the flower buds are showing colour, move the pots indoors. Once blooms have faded, cut off spent stems and water as needed until the foliage dies down.

Indoors
If growing hyacinths indoors, choose a container 10–15cm (4–6in) deep but plant the bulbs just below the surface of the compost. (In pots without drainage holes, bulb fibre can be used intead of compost.) Water after planting, allow to drain and then transfer the pot to a cool, dark position. The pots can be placed inside a black plastic bag and put into a shed, cold frame or similar place with a temperature of around 4°C (40°F). Check from time to time to see if shoots have emerged. Once shoots emerge (this usually takes around 10–12 weeks) and reach 2.5–5cm (1–2in) in height, bring the pot into the light, gradually increasing the amount of light as the shoots green up. As buds appear, give them as much sunlight as possible.

In glass
Hyacinths can also be grown in a glass or ceramic container that has a narrow neck. Sometimes you can buy a purpose-built container, usually plastic, that has the top cut into segments so that the bulb sits neatly on it. Fill the container with water to just below the rim. Choose a good-sized bulb, then rest it on top of the rim of the container so that the base of the bulb is in water. Place the container in a cool, dark place and leave it there until large numbers of roots have formed and the flower bud is starting to emerge, when they can be brought into the light. These bulbs are unlikely to regrow and may be discarded after flowering.

HYACINTHUS AT A GLANCE

Sweetly scented, densely packed flower spikes, ideal for growing indoors or outside. Frost hardy.

		RECOMMENDED VARIETIES
JAN	flowering	'Amsterdam'
FEB	flowering	'Anna Marie'
MAR	flowering	'Blue Giant'
APR	flowering	'City of Haarlem'
MAY	/	'Delft Blue'
JUN	/	'Gipsy Queen'
JULY	/	'Jan Bos'
AUG	/	'L'Innocence'
SEPT	plant	'Lord Balfour'
OCT	plant	'Mont Blanc'
NOV	/	'Queen of the Pinks'
DEC	flowering	

1.

2.

4.

5.

HYACINTH
(*HYACINTHUS ORIENTALIS*)

The dense clusters of flowers on hyacinth spikes come in a wonderful range of clear colours.

1. 'L'Innocence' is a pure white hyacinth first raised in 1863 and still very popular today.

2. Pale rose-pink 'Lady Derby' blooms reliably in the garden or in containers.

3. The subtle stripes on the petals of the violet-blue 'Ostara' make this a very attractive hyacinth.

4. 'Amsterdam' is an unusually deep pink colour. For a real crimson hyacinth select 'Jan Bos'.

5. Clear primrose yellow 'City of Haarlem' breaks away from the traditional pink or blue.

6. This soft mauve-blue hyacinth is still pretty as the flower fades.

3.

6.

HYMENOCALLIS
Spider lily, Peruvian daffodil

THE WHITE *or cream flowers of spider lilies are something like an exotic daffodil, with an attractive fragrance.*

HYMENOCALLIS CAN *be grown outside in reasonably sheltered gardens, but the bulbs should be lifted in autumn to ensure survival.*

FEATURES

Spider lilies are native to various parts of North and South America. They produce broad, strap-shaped, deep green leaves and fascinating, lightly fragrant flowers which are carried on a stout stem. The flower has a trumpet-shaped central cup with long, narrow, petal-like segments surrounding it; flowers are usually white but can be yellow or cream. Hymenocallis can be grown in a sheltered, sunny position outside, but is often treated as a greenhouse or conservatory plant. All spider lilies can be container grown. *H.* x *festalis, H. narcissiflora* and the cultivar 'Sulphur Queen' are the deciduous varieties most often grown, while the more difficult to find *H. littoralis* and *H. speciosa* are the most popular of the evergreen species. Hymenocallis is sometimes also listed as ismene.

HYMENOCALLIS AT A GLANCE

A rather tender bulb bearing unusual fragrant blooms like exotic daffodils. Can also be grown as a conservatory plant.

		RECOMMENDED VARIETIES
JAN	/	
FEB	/	'Advance'
MAR	plant (indoors) 🖐	'Sulphur Queen'
APR	/	
MAY	🖐(outdoors)/flowering 🌼	*Hymenocallis* x *festalis:*
JUN	flowering 🌼	'Zwanenburg'
JULY	/	
AUG	flowering 🌼	
SEPT	/	
OCT	/	
NOV	/	
DEC	/	

CONDITIONS

Aspect Grows in full sun or light shade with shelter from strong wind.

Site In sheltered gardens hymenocallis can be grown outside in beds and borders or containers. In cold areas, it is best grown as a greenhouse or conservatory plant. Soil must be free draining. Use soilless potting compost for pots.

GROWING METHOD

Planting For growing in containers, plant bulbs in spring with the neck of the bulb just below the soil surface, using one of the large bulbs per 15cm (6in) pot. Outdoors, plant in May, burying the bulbs 12.5cm (5in) deep.

Feeding High potash liquid fertiliser can be applied as buds form. Mulching around plants with well-rotted organic matter also supplies nutrients. Water sparingly until the shoots show, then water regularly through the growing season.

Problems No specific problems are usually experienced.

FLOWERING

Season The fragrant spider lilies are produced in early summer indoors, mid to late summer outside.

Cutting Makes a delightful and unusual cut flower.

AFTER FLOWERING

Requirements Allow the foliage to die down after flowering; lift outdoor bulbs and store in dry peat in a frost-free place over winter. Leave potted plants dry in their containers over winter and repot the following spring.

IPHEION UNIFLORUM
Spring star flower

SPRING STAR FLOWER is an ideal edging plant for a sunny garden and it can be left undisturbed for several years.

THE SOFT LILAC of the flowers makes spring star flower very versatile as it blends into most garden colour schemes.

FEATURES

This low-growing plant makes an ideal edging but should be planted in large drifts wherever it is grown to produce its best effect. Tolerant of rather tough growing conditions, it is most suitable for filling pockets in a rockery or growing towards the front of a herbaceous border. It also makes a good container plant. It has grey-green, narrow, strappy leaves which smell strongly of onions when crushed; the pale blue, starry, lightly scented flowers are carried on stems 15cm (6in) or so high. There are several varieties available with flowers ranging in colour from white to deep violet-blue.

IPHEION AT A GLANCE

A low-growing bulb with a profusion of starry blue or white flowers in spring.

		RECOMMENDED VARIETIES
JAN	/	
FEB	/	'Album'
MAR	flowering	'Alberto Castello'
APR	flowering	'Froyle Mill'
MAY	flowering	'Rolf Fiedler'
JUN	/	'Wisley Blue'
JULY	/	
AUG	/	
SEPT	plant	
OCT	plant	
NOV	/	
DEC	/	

CONDITIONS

Aspect Grows best in full sun but tolerates light shade for part of the day.

Site Good for a rockery, border or container. Ipheion needs well-drained soil. It will grow on fairly poor soils but growth will be better on soils enriched with organic matter.

GROWING METHOD

Planting Plant bulbs 5cm (2in) deep and the same distance apart in autumn.

Feeding Apply some balanced fertiliser after flowers have finished. Water regularly during dry spells while plants are in leaf and bloom.

Problems No specific problems are usually experienced with this bulb.

FLOWERING

Season The starry flowers appear from early spring to mid-spring.

Cutting Flowers are too short to cut for all but a miniature vase but they may last a few days in water.

AFTER FLOWERING

Requirements Shear off spent flower stems and remove the old foliage once it has died down. If clumps become overcrowded and fail to flower well, they can be lifted in autumn, divided, and replanted immediately.

IRIS – BULBOUS TYPES

Irises

THE LOW-GROWING *flowers of* Iris danfordiae *appear very early in the year – usually February or March.*

SEVERAL DIFFERENT *cultivars of* Iris reticulata *are available, in varying shades of blue with yellow markings.*

FEATURES

There are many species of these irises, which have true bulbs as storage organs, unlike the creeping rhizomes of their larger cousins. The leaves are not arranged in the typical fan of sword shapes like rhizomatous irises, but are usually narrow and lance shaped, or rolled. The flowers have the typical iris form with six petals, three inner ones (standards), and three outer ones (falls). The falls are often brightly marked or veined. Many species and varieties are blue with yellow markings on the falls; some types are yellow with brown or green speckling on the falls and others are white with yellow markings. The blue varieties come in many shades, from deep violet and purple through to pale China blue.

Many bulbous irises are early-flowering dwarf forms suitable for growing on rockeries or at the front of beds: they are also excellent for shallow pots ('pans') in the greenhouse or alpine house. Other types are taller and flower in summer; they are valuable for herbaceous and mixed borders, and are particularly good for cutting for flower arrangements. There are also some spring-flowering irises which are far less commonly grown than the other groups.

POPULAR SPECIES

Bulbous irises can be split into three main groups: Reticulata irises, Xiphium irises and Juno irises.

Reticulata These irises have bulbs with a netted tunic around them which gives them their group name. They are dwarf, growing to around 15cm (6in) high, and the flowers appear early in the year, usually in February and March. *I. danfordiae* has lightly fragrant flowers whose yellow petals are speckled with greenish brown. *I. reticulata* also has fragrant flowers: the petals are thinner than those of *I. danfordiae* and are blue or purple with yellow markings. Several different cultivars are available. The flowers of *I. histriodes* and its cultivars are larger and have short stems; they are deep to light blue, with dark blue, white and yellow markings. The flowers open before the leaves reach their full height.

Xiphium This group of summer-flowering irises is popular and easily grown. It consists of Dutch irises, flowering in early summer, in white, yellow or blue with contrasting markings; English irises, flowering in early to mid-summer in shades of white, blue or purple; and Spanish irises, flowering in mid-summer in various shades of white, blue, purple and yellow.

Juno The Juno irises are not as well-known as the other bulbous types, probably because they are more difficult to grow well. The group includes *I. bucharica*, bearing yellow or white flowers with yellow falls, and *I. graeberiana*, which has lavender flowers with a white crest on the falls. These two are among the easiest Juno irises to grow: others include *I. fosteriana*, *I. magnifica* and *I. rosenbachiana*, which do best in an alpine house.

WHEN EXAMINED closely, the lightly fragrant flowers of Iris danfordiae *can been seen to have attractive freckling in the throat.*

'KATHERINE HODGKIN', a cultivar of Iris histrioides, *is per-haps the most sought-after of all the dwarf irises.*

CONDITIONS

Aspect
Site
All bulbous irises like open, sunny, positions. Reticulatas are good for rock gardens, raised beds, or containers: Xiphiums and Junos for sunny, sheltered borders. Soil needs to be well drained; Juno irises require a soil containing plenty of well-rotted organic matter.

GROWING METHOD

Planting
Plant Reticulatas 7.5cm (3in) deep and 10cm (4in) apart. Xiphiums are planted 10–15cm (4–6in) deep and 15cm (6in) apart, and Juno irises are planted 5cm (2in) deep and 20cm (8in) apart, taking care not to damage the brittle, fleshy roots. They are all planted in autumn, in September or October.

Feeding
Supplementary feeding is not normally necessary.

Problems
Bulbs may rot in overwet soil. Bulbous irises in warmer areas of the country may be affected by iris ink disease, causing black streaks on the bulb and yellow blotches on the leaves. Destroy affected bulbs.

FLOWERING

Season
Reticulata irises flower in February and March, Junos in April and May, and Xiphiums in June and July.

Cutting
The Xiphiums make excellent, long-lasting cut flowers.

AFTER FLOWERING

Requirements Remove faded flowers. Most bulbous irises are best left undisturbed for as long as possible; they can be increased by lifting and dividing the bulbs after flowering when necessary. Juno irises should not be divided until the foliage has died down, and must be handled very carefully. Spanish irises of the Xiphium group benefit from being lifted when the foliage has died down and replanted in September; this helps the bulbs to ripen.

BULBOUS IRIS AT A GLANCE

A varied group of plants with colourful flowers in early spring or in summer. Good for a range of situations.

		RECOMMENDED VARIETIES
JAN	flowering	Reticulata group:
FEB	flowering	*I. danfordiae*
MAR	flowering	*I. reticulata* 'Katharine Hodgkin'
APR	flowering	*I. histrioides* 'Major'
MAY	flowering	Xiphium group:
JUN	flowering	'Bronze Queen'
JULY	flowering	'Excelsior'
AUG	/	'Ideal'
SEPT	plant	Juno group:
OCT	plant	*I. bucharica*
NOV	/	*I. graeberiana*
DEC	/	

IRIS – RHIZOMATOUS TYPES

IRIS WAS THE Greek god of the the rainbow, and this plant is aptly named as there are irises in every colour of the spectrum.

WATER IRIS (Iris pseudoacorus) is a tall grower that needs to be planted in water or permanently wet soil.

FEATURES

Irises comprise a very large plant group of over 200 species. Some grow from bulbs (see the previous two pages): those covered here grow from rhizomes. They have stiff, sword-shaped leaves and carry their colourful flowers on tall, stiff stems in spring and early summer. Iris flowers have six petals; three inner, vertical ones, (standards), and three outer ones, which curve outwards (falls). The colour range is very varied, covering blue, purple, lavender, yellow, rose and white; many of the flowers are bicoloured, and attractively marked. Rhizomatous irises contain several different groups, the most popular of which are bearded, Japanese and Siberian irises. **Bearded irises** have large, very showy flowers with a short, bristly 'beard' on the falls; dwarf cultivars are also available. **Japanese irises** have unusual flat-faced flowers, and **Siberian irises** have delicate flowers with finer petals.

CONDITIONS

Aspect	Rhizomatous irises like a position in full sun, but with protection from strong winds.
Site	Excellent plants for the middle to back of a mixed or herbaceous border. Bearded irises like a slightly alkaline, well-drained soil: Japanese and Siberian irises need moisture-retentive, humus-rich loam.

GROWING METHOD

Planting	Usually sold as container-grown plants in growth. Plant shallowly, with the rhizome barely covered, in late summer.
Feeding	Supplementary feeding is rarely necessary. Ensure moisture-loving types are never allowed to dry out during the growing season.
Problems	Slugs and snails can be troublesome. Use covered slug bait where necessary, or hand pick the pests after dark.

FLOWERING

Season	Flowers are carried in early summer.
Cutting	Make lovely cut flowers.

AFTER FLOWERING

Requirements	Cut off spent flower stems. Every few years, lift the rhizomes after flowering, cut them into sections each containing a strong, healthy fan of leaves, and replant, discarding the old, woody, worn out portions of rhizome.

RHIZOMATOUS IRIS AT A GLANCE

Stately border plants with fans of sword-shaped leaves and tall, attractively marked flowers in summer.

JAN	/	**RECOMMENDED VARIETIES**
FEB	/	
MAR	/	*Bearded irises:*
APR	/	'Black Swan'
MAY	flowering	'Rocket'
JUN	flowering	'White City'
JULY	flowering	*Siberian irises:*
AUG	/	'Sparkling Rose'
SEPT	plant	'Caesar'
OCT	/	'Perry's Blue'
NOV	/	*Japanese irises:*
DEC	/	'Rose Queen'
		'Moonlight Waves'

IRIS UNGUICULARIS
Winter iris, Algerian iris

THE FULL BEAUTY of this iris can be seen in close up. Many iris have fine veining or feathering on their petals.

A LARGE PATCH of Algerian iris gives a great lift to the garden in winter. Even if flowers come singly their appearance is still a joy.

FEATURES

This beardless, rhizomatous iris is different to all others in its group because it flowers throughout the winter. The lovely little fragrant flowers rarely exceed 20cm (8in) in height and may be hidden by the stiff, grassy foliage. They are ideal for cutting and taking indoors, where their sweet scent may be almost overpowering at times.

The flowers of the species are deep lavender with creamy yellow centres deeply veined in violet. There are some cultivars available, including a white form, one or two varieties in particularly deep shades of blue, one in a pale silvery lilac, and a dwarf form. A large single clump of this iris is effective but in the right position it could be mass planted to good effect.

I. UNGUICULARIS AT A GLANCE

A low-growing iris valuable for its sweetly scented flowers which appear throughout the winter.

		RECOMMENDED VARIETIES
JAN	flowering 🌷	'Abington Purple'
FEB	flowering 🌷	'Alba'
MAR	plant ✍	'Bob Thompson'
APR	/	'Mary Barnard'
MAY	/	'Oxford Dwarf'
JUN	/	'Walter Butt'
JULY	/	
AUG	/	
SEPT	/	
OCT	/	
NOV	flowering 🌷	
DEC	flowering 🌷	

CONDITIONS

Aspect Needs a reasonably sheltered position because of its flowering time. The rhizomes must be exposed to a summer baking if plants are to flower well, so a position in full sun is essential.

Site Grow in beds or borders where it will be able to spread – plants can be invasive. Soil must be well drained. If it is very poor, dig in quantities of well-decayed manure or compost ahead of planting time.

GROWING METHOD

Planting Plant rhizomes in spring with the top at or just below soil level. Container-grown plants in growth can also be bought and planted virtually year round in suitable weather.

Feeding Supplementary feeding is generally unnecessary. Water the plants in spring and autumn if conditions are dry, but do not water in summer.

Problems Slugs and snails will often attack the flowers. Use slug pellets if necessary.

FLOWERING

Season Flowers are produced any time from late autumn through winter.

Cutting The flowers make a lovely indoor decoration.

AFTER FLOWERING

Requirements Cut off spent flowers and tidy up foliage when necessary. Little other attention is required. Crowded plants can be divided in spring.

IXIA
Corn lily

EACH TALL SPIKE of corn lily produces dozens of flowers. These are still producing blooms despite the many fading and falling ones.

PALEST TURQUOISE FLOWERS make this lovely corn lily (Ixia viridiflora) *a favourite although its corms are not always easy to buy.*

FEATURES

This plant produces starry flowers in a stunning range of colours including white, cream, yellow, orange, red, cerise and magenta. Hybrid varieties are the most popular, but the sought-after *I. viridiflora* has duck-egg blue flowers with a dark centre. The narrow, grass-like foliage may be 30–50cm (12–20in) high while the wiry-stemmed flower spikes stand clear of the leaves. Corn lilies are a great addition to the garden. Being fairly tall they should be planted towards the back of a bed or among other bulbs and perennials. Although colours can be mixed, a better effect is obtained by planting blocks of one colour.

IXIA AT A GLANCE

A rather tender plant with masses of colourful, starry flowers on slender stems.

		RECOMMENDED VARIETIES
JAN	/	
FEB	/	'Blue Bird'
MAR	plant	'Mabel'
APR	plant	'Rose Emperor'
MAY	flowering	'Venus'
JUN	flowering	
JULY	flowering	
AUG	/	
SEPT	/	
OCT	plant (indoors)	
NOV	/	
DEC	/	

CONDITIONS

Aspect   Prefers full sun all day but with shelter from strong wind.

Site   A good border plant in reasonably mild districts. In colder areas it can be grown in containers on a sheltered patio or in a conservatory. Needs well-drained soil.

GROWING METHOD

Planting   Plant corms in the open garden in spring, about 5cm (2in) deep and 8–10cm (3–4in) apart. Plant in pots for the conservatory in autumn.

Fertilising   Apply balanced liquid fertiliser in early spring to increase the size of the blooms. In dry conditions, water if necessary in spring once the shoots are growing strongly.

Problems   No specific pest or disease problems are usually experienced, though corms may rot in overwet soil.

FLOWERING

Season   Flowers from late spring to mid-summer.

Cutting   Flowers can be cut for the vase but will probably give better value in the garden.

AFTER FLOWERING

Requirements   In all but the mildest gardens, lift the corms once the foliage has died down and store them in a dry place for replanting in spring.

LACHENALIA ALOIDES
Cape cowslip

STIFF FLOWER SPIKES of yellow and red tubular bells are the hallmark of Lachenalia aloides.

CAPE COWSLIPS need a cool room to grow well. In the right conditions they make excellent winter-flowering house plants.

FEATURES

Also known as 'soldier boys' because of its upright, neat and orderly habit, this bulb is grown as a house plant to produce its colourful bell-like flowers in midwinter. The rather stiff leaves grow to about 15cm (6in) high and are dark green, often spotted with purple. The 20–30cm (8–12in) spikes of 20 or so tubular flowers stand well above the foliage and remain colourful for several weeks. Individual blooms are yellow or orange-red, marked with red, green or purple; they are often a deeper colour in bud, becoming paler as the flowers open. There are several different varieties with subtly varying shades to the flowers.

LACHENALIA AT A GLANCE

A tender bulb grown as a house or greenhouse plant for its spikes of yellow or orange tubular flowers in winter.

JAN	flowering 🌿	RECOMMENDED VARIETIES
FEB	flowering 🌿	
MAR	flowering 🌿	*Lachenalia aloides:*
APR	/	'Aurea'
MAY	/	'Lutea'
JUN	/	'Nelsonii'
JULY	/	'Quadricolor'
AUG	plant 🌱	
SEPT	plant 🌱	*Lachenalia bulbifera:*
OCT	/	'George'
NOV	/	
DEC	/	

CONDITIONS

Aspect   Needs a very brightly lit spot; will stand direct sun for part of the day.

Site   Grow on a bright windowsill in a cool room, or in a cool greenhouse or conservatory. Lachenalia does not like centrally heated rooms.

GROWING METHOD

Planting   Plant bulbs in late summer or early autumn, growing six to a 12.5cm (5in.) pot. Set them just below the surface of the compost.

Feeding   Apply high potash liquid fertiliser every 14 days or so from when the buds appear. Water regularly while plants are in flower.

Problems   Overwatering or poorly drained compost will cause the bulbs to rot.

FLOWERING

Season   Flowers appear between midwinter and early spring.

Cutting   Not suitable for cutting.

AFTER FLOWERING

Requirements   Cut off spent lachenalia flower stems. Continue to water until early summer, then gradually stop watering and allow the pot to dry out until the following autumn, when the bulbs can be shaken out and repotted in fresh compost.

LEUCOJUM
Snowflake

THE WHITE BELLS *with their fresh green dots at the end of each petal make* Leucojum vernum *particularly evocative of spring.*

PREFERRING SHADE *and moist soil, spring snowflake is one of the easiest bulbs to grow. This plant is typical of an established clump.*

FEATURES

Easily grown snowflakes have clusters of white, bell-shaped flowers, each petal bearing a bright green spot on its tip. Foliage is a rich, deep green and bulbs multiply readily to form good sized clumps in a few years.

There are three types of snowflake; spring snowflake (*Leucojum vernum*), summer snowflake (*L. aestivum*) and autumn snowflake (*L. autumnale*). The spring snowflake flowers in February or March, while the summer snowflake, despite its name, usually flowers in late spring. Spring snowflake reaches a height of around 20cm (8in); summer snowflake up to 60cm (24in) and autumn snowflake 15cm (6in), with very fine, narrow foliage. The flowers have a passing resemblance to snowdrops, but are easily distinguished by their rounded, bell shape and taller growth.

LEUCOJUM AT A GLANCE

Delicate looking plants with white bells tipped with green, appearing in spring or early autumn. Hardy.

		RECOMMENDED VARIETIES
JAN	/	
FEB	flowering	*Leucojum aestivum:*
MAR	flowering	'Gravetye Giant'
APR	flowering	
MAY	flowering	*Leucojum autumnale:*
JUN	/	'Cobb's Variety'
JULY	/	'Pulchellum'
AUG	/	
SEPT	plant / flower	*Leucojum vernum:*
OCT	plant	'Carpathicum'
NOV	/	'Vagneri'
DEC	/	

CONDITIONS

Aspect Grows well in sun but also happy in shade or in dappled sunlight. Autumn snowflakes prefer an open, sunny position.

Site Low-growing species are excellent for rock gardens or the front of borders; taller summer snowflakes towards the middle of a border. Spring and summer snowflakes prefer a moisture-retentive soil enriched with organic matter: autumn snowflake needs light, free-draining soil.

GROWING METHOD

Planting Plant bulbs 7.5cm (3in) deep and 10–20cm (4–8in) apart in late summer or early autumn.

Feeding An annual mulching with decayed manure or compost after bulbs have died down should provide adequate nutrients. Keep the soil for spring and summer snowflakes moist throughout the growing season.

Problems No specific problems are known.

FLOWERING

Season Spring snowflake flowers between midwinter and early spring; summer snowflake mid to late spring and autumn snowflake in September.

Cutting Best enjoyed in the garden.

AFTER FLOWERING

Requirements Remove spent flower stems. Divide crowded clumps when the foliage dies down, and replant immediately.

LILIUM
Lily

THIS BURNT ORANGE HYBRID shows the characteristic dark spotting in its throat. Lilies make excellent cut flowers.

WHITE LILIES are traditionally symbols of purity. Lilium regale is one of the most popular species, and its flowers are very strongly scented.

FEATURES

Lilies are tall, stately plants that carry a number of large, trumpet-shaped blooms on each flowering stem. Flowering stems may be anywhere from about 60cm (2ft) to over 2m (6ft) high. There are 80–90 species of lily and many hundreds of cultivars, so it is difficult to outline their requirements concisely. Lily flowers are often fragrant and the main colour range includes white, yellow, pink, red and orange – many have spotted or streaked petals. A fairly small range of lily bulbs is usually available in garden centres in autumn and these should be planted as soon as possible after their arrival: lily bulbs have no tunic or outer covering and so can dry out unless they are carefully handled. For a greater range of species and hybrids you will need to contact specialist growers and mail order suppliers. Many lily enthusiasts belong to societies devoted to learning more about the enormous range of types available and their cultivation.

Types
Some of the more popular species grown are *L. auratum*, golden-rayed lily, which has white petals with gold bands; *L. candidum*, Madonna lily, which is pure white; *L. martagon*, Turk's cap lily, with fully recurved, dark red petals with dark spots; *L. regale*, the regal lily, with white flowers which have purple backs to the petals and a yellow base; *L. speciosum* which has white petals with a deep pink centre and reddish spots; and *L. tigrinum*, tiger lily, dark orange with black spots and revurving petals. As well as the species, many hybrid varieties are grown, which are classified into a number of groups. Among the most popular are the Asiatic hybrids, short to medium height, with upward-facing flowers produced early in the season; and the Oriental hybrids, which are taller and more refined, with nodding, strongly scented blooms. Asiatic hybrids are ideal for pots and are available pot grown throughout the summer.

CONDITIONS

Aspect
The ideal situation is a sunny position with a little dappled shade during part of the day. They need protection from strong wind.

Site
Lilies grow well when mixed with other plants that will shade their roots, in a bed or border, or in containers. Plant them where their perfume can be appreciated. Soil must be well drained with a high organic content. Dig in copious amounts of well-rotted manure or compost a month or so before planting.

GROWING METHOD

Planting
Plant 10–23cm (4–9in) deep and 23–38cm (9–15in) or so apart in autumn or early spring. Bulbs must not be bruised or allowed to dry out, and they should be planted as soon as possible after purchase. Apply a layer of compost or manure to the soil surface as a mulch after planting. Your stock of lilies can be increased by bulb scales, bulbils or offsets, according to type: see page 11 for more details on propagation.

THE GOLDEN-RAYED lily of Japan, Lilium auratum, *carries its attractively speckled, reflexing flowers late in the summer.*

MASSES OF BLOOMS, with buds still to open, make this yellow lily a great asset for the summer garden.

Feeding   If the soil contains plenty of organic matter these plants should not need a lot of feeding. Apply a slow-release granular fertiliser as growth starts and after flowering. Water regularly during dry spells but avoid overwatering which may rot the bulbs.

Problems   Most problems with lilies result from poor cultivation or unsuitable growing conditions. Grey mould (botrytis) can be a problem in cool, humid conditions, especially if plants are overwatered or if air circulation is poor. The small, bright red lily beetle and their larvae can cause a lot of damage in some areas:

control them with a contact insecticide and clear away plant debris in which the adults overwinter.

FLOWERING

Season   Lilies flower some time between early summer and autumn with many flowering in middle to late summer. Flowering time depends on the species and, to some extent, the conditions.

Cutting   Lilies make wonderful and very long lasting cut flowers. Cut them when flowers are just open or all buds are rounded and fully coloured. Don't cut right to the bottom of the stem – retain some leaves on the lower part. Change water frequently and cut off spent flowers from the cluster to allow the other buds to develop fully.

AFTER FLOWERING

Requirements   Remove spent flower stems as they finish blooming. Remove only the flowering stem and leave as much foliage as possible. Don't be in a hurry to cut back yellowing growth too soon: allow the plant to die back naturally and mulch with chipped bark for the winter. Bulbs are best left in the ground for several years. When they are lifted they must be divided and replanted at-once, as having no tunic on the bulb means they dry out very quickly. If they can't be planted at once, store them in damp sphagnum moss or peat.

LILIUM AT A GLANCE

Stately plants with trumpet-shaped, usually intensely fragrant flowers on tall spikes.

		RECOMMENDED VARIETIES
JAN	/	
FEB	/	'Apollo'
MAR	/	'Barcelona'
APR	/	'Casa Blanca'
MAY	/	'Corsage'
JUN	flowering 🌸	'Enchantment'
JULY	flowering 🌸	'Green Dragon'
AUG	flowering 🌸/plant 🖐	'Mrs R. O. Backhouse'
SEPT	flowering 🌸/plant 🖐	'Orange Triumph'
OCT	plant 🖐	'Shuksan'
NOV	plant 🖐	'Tamara'
DEC	/	

MORAEA
Peacock iris, butterfly iris

IT IS EASY to see how this pretty bulb got its common name of peacock iris. Iridescent blue spots are sharply defined against the white petals.

THE FOLIAGE of peacock iris looks unpromising, as it is sparse and grass-like, but the 'floating' flowers are worth waiting for.

FEATURES

Of the 120 species of *Moraea*, most come from South Africa with others native to tropical Africa and Madagascar. Few are in cultivation but it is worth seeking out this unusual plant from specialist bulb growers. All grow from corms and some, such as *M. spathulata*, grow only a single leaf, which may be 20–50cm (8–20in) high.

Flowers are like those of irises, with three showy outer petals and three smaller, rather insignificant inner ones. The commonest species is *M. spathulata*, with bright yellow, summer flowers on 60cm (2ft) stems. *Moraea aristata* has white flowers with a large blue blotch at the base of the outer petals, while *M. villosa* bears flowers in a range of colours with a blue blotch on the petals.

Plant peacock iris in groups for the best effect.

MORAEA AT A GLANCE

An uncommon bulb with iris-like flowers, often strikingly marked. Needs a warm, sunny position.

		RECOMMENDED SPECIES
JAN	/	
FEB	/	*Moraea aristata*
MAR	/	M. *bellendenii*
APR	plant 🖐	M. *gawleri*
MAY	/	M. *spathulata*
JUN	flowering 🌸	
JULY	flowering 🌸	
AUG	flowering 🌸	
SEPT	/	
OCT	/	
NOV	/	
DEC	/	

CONDITIONS

Aspect Moraea needs full sun all day.
Site A warm, sunny and sheltered position is necessary. This corm needs well-drained soil with plenty of decayed organic matter incorporated into it before planting. Moraea also makes an attractive plant for the conservatory or home when grown in containers. Use John Innes or soilless potting compost.

GROWING METHOD

Planting Plant corms 5cm (2in) deep and 20cm (8in) apart in spring.
Feeding Performance is improved by applying a balanced fertiliser as flower buds appear. Container-grown plants should be liquid fed every three weeks or so through the growing season. Water in dry conditions, but take care not to make the soil too wet or the corms will be liable to rot.
Problems No specific pest or disease problems are known for this plant.

FLOWERING

Season Flowers throughout the summer.
Cutting Not suitable for cutting.

AFTER FLOWERING

Requirements Cut off spent flower stems unless you want to obtain seed from them. In autumn, lift the corms and store them in a dry place over winter, ready for replanting the following spring.

MUSCARI
Grape hyacinth

THE FEATHERY *violet heads of* Muscari comosum *'Plumosum'*
make this showy variety quite different from other grape hyacinths.

ROYAL BLUE *grape hyacinths here border a garden of daffodils and*
pop up from among the groundcover of snow-in-summer.

FEATURES

Vigorous and easy to grow, grape hyacinths
have blue flowers of varying intensity. There
are several species and named varieties
available, including the double 'Blue Spike'
and the feathery 'Plumosum'. *Muscari aucheri*
(*M. tubergenianum*) is known as 'Oxford and
Cambridge' because it has pale blue flowers at
the top of the spike and dark blue at the base.
Grape hyacinths are a great foil for other
bright spring-flowering bulbs such as tulips or
ranunculus. Flowers are lightly scented and are
carried on a stem about 10–20cm (4–8in) tall.
This plant gives the most impact when
planted in drifts: in large gardens where there
is space it can easily be naturalised in grass or
under deciduous trees.

MUSCARI AT A GLANCE

Pretty, easy-to-grow, little bulbs with short spikes of intense
blue bells in spring.

JAN	/	
FEB	/	
MAR	flowering 🌱	
APR	flowering 🌱	
MAY	flowering 🌱	
JUN	/	
JULY	/	
AUG	/	
SEPT	plant ✍	
OCT	plant ✍	
NOV	/	
DEC	/	

RECOMMENDED VARIETIES

Muscari armeniacum:
  'Blue Spike'
  'Early Giant'

Muscari azureum:
  'Album'

Muscari comosum:
  'Plumosum'

CONDITIONS

Aspect   Best in full sun or dappled sunlight such as is
found under deciduous trees.
Site   Useful on rockeries, in the front of borders and
for naturalising under trees, but the plants can
be invasive. Muscari needs well-drained soil,
preferably with plenty of organic matter
incorporated before planting.

GROWING METHOD

Planting   Plant the bulbs about 7.5cm (3in) deep and
10cm (4in) apart in late summer or early
autumn.
Feeding   Supplementary feeding is not normally
necessary, but a light sprinkling of general
fertiliser after flowering helps to ensure good
growth. Watering is not normally necessary
unless the weather is exceptionally dry.
Problems   No specific problems are known.

FLOWERING

Season   Flowers appear in early to mid-spring.
Cutting   Although not often used as a cut flower, it
lasts in water quite well if picked when half
the flowers on the stem are open.

AFTER FLOWERING

Requirements   Remove spent flower stems if required. Bulbs
can be divided every 3–4 years in autumn,
replanting immediately. The foliage appears in
the winter, long before the flowers.

NARCISSUS
Daffodil and narcissus

MODERN HYBRID DAFFODILS come in a wide range of forms, including double-flowered varieties and varieties with split coronas.

SUNSHINE YELLOW, this group of smaller growing daffodil cultivars lights up the late winter garden.

FEATURES

Daffodils are probably the best known and most widely grown of all bulbs and to many they are the true indicator of spring. They look wonderful mass planted in the garden or naturalised in grass, but they also make great pot plants and excellent cut flowers. The best-known colour is yellow, but there are also flowers in shades of white, cream, orange and pink. The trumpet, or cup, is often a different colour to the petals and may be bicoloured. There are many species and cultivars and the genus *Narcissus* has been divided into 12 different groups, depending on the form and size of the flowers. The height varies from 7.5–50cm (3–20in), depending on variety.

Trumpet   The trumpet (cup) is at least as long as the petals, and there is one flower per stem.

Large cupped   Cup is shorter than, but at least one-third of, the length of the petals. One flower per stem.

Small cupped   The cup is less than one-third of the length of the petals; flowers usually carried singly.

Double   Double or semi-double flowers carried single or in small groups. The whole flower may be double, or just the cup.

Triandrus   Two to six pendant flowers with reflexed petals per stem.

Cyclamineus   Slightly pendant flowers with long trumpets and strongly reflexed petals, usually one per stem.

Jonquilla   Several flowers per stem, with short cups. Sweetly scented.

Tazetta   Half hardy. Very fragrant flowers in clusters of 10 or more per stem. Early flowering.

Poeticus   Small red or orange cup and broad white petals, usually one or two per stem. Often strongly fragrant. Late flowering.

Wild   A varied group containing the species and natural varieties found in the wild.

Split cupped   The cup is split to varying degrees for at least one-third to half its length.

Miscellaneous   Hybrids which do not fit into any of the other divisions.

CONDITIONS

Aspect   These bulbs grow best in a sunny spot or under deciduous trees where they will receive sun in the early spring.

Site   Grow narcissi in beds and borders, on rockeries, or in containers for the patio or in the home. Soil must be well drained, ideally with some well-rotted organic matter dug in a month or so before planting.

GROWING METHOD

Planting   Planting depth will vary greatly according to the size of the bulb. Plant so that the nose is covered to twice the height of the bulb, in September or October. Plant as early as possible for the best results.
Continued on page 82

1.

2.

5.

6.

7.

3.

4.

8.

9.

DAFFODILS

There are many daffodil cultivars with wonderful variety in form and colour. Yellow is most common colour but some have white or pinkish petals or cups.

1. 'Flower Record' displays the characteristics of N. poeticus, *which is in its breeding.*

2. Bright, clear yellow 'Meeting' is a fine example of modern double daffodils.

3. 'E. E. Morbey', dating from the 1930s, has a particularly pretty centre to its orange cup.

4. 'Ice Follies' has white petals. The flared lemon cup fades as it ages.

5. Simplicity of form and white purity make 'Mount Hood' a classic variety.

6. Reddish-orange inner petals on double-flowered 'Tahiti' make it a very showy addition to the garden.

7. The yellow and white centre of 'White Lion' demonstrates another style of double daffodil.

8. Soft, pretty 'Mrs Oscar Ronalds' has a long pink cup and white petals.

9. 'King Alfred', raised about 1890, is possibly the most widely grown of all yellow daffodils.

1.

2.

4.

3.

5.

6.

JONQUILS
(*NARCISSUS*)

Jonquils, with their multiple flowers
on each stem, are lovely flowers.
These pages show just some of the
cultivars available.

1. 'Erlicheer' is a beautiful, double
jonquil with a rich creamy colour
and heavy perfume.

2. 'Soleil d'Or', with bright yellow
petals and orange cups, often flowers
during midwinter.

3. 'Cheerfulness', dating from 1923, is
an aptly named late bloomer.

4. The subtle cream on white colouring
of 'Pearl' gives a delicate appearance.

5. Sturdy growth and reliable flowering
make 'Grand Monarque' a good
choice for warm areas.

6. 'Cragford' has a flattened orange cup
with red rim, typical of N. poeticus
cultivars.

THE ESSENCE OF SPRING BEAUTY is captured in this drift of mixed daffodils and delicate white blossom. As the planting has been kept to the edge of the lawn, the grass can be mown while still allowing the bulb foliage to die down naturally.

Continued from page 77

Feeding   Feed with a balanced fertiliser in early spring. Plants can be given a liquid feed after the flowers have faded. Watering may be necessary in very dry spells, particularly once flowering has finished.

Problems   Basal rot can occur in storage; destroy bulbs with any sign of softening or rot at planting time. Similar symptoms can be caused by stem eelworm; these bulbs should also be destroyed by burning. Narcissus fly lays eggs near the necks of the bulbs; these hatch into larvae that tunnel into the bulb and weaken or destroy it. Bulbs in light shade are less susceptible to attack. Pull soil up round the necks of the bulbs after flowering to discourage egg laying.

FLOWERING

Season   Depending on area and variety, flowers may be carried anywhere from midwinter to early summer. Bulbs indoors may be brought into flower for Christmas or earlier; specially treated bulbs are available to ensure early flowering.

Cutting   This excellent cut flower should last a week with frequent water changes, or with the use of proprietary cut flower additives. For longest vase life pick daffodils when the buds are about to burst open or as soon as they are fully open. Cut, don't pull, the stems as low as possible. Cut off any white section at the base of the stem. Don't mix daffodils with other flowers until they have spent a day in a vase on their own as their slimy sap may reduce the vase life of other blooms.

AFTER FLOWERING

Requirements   Spent flowers should be removed before they set seed. Allow foliage to die down naturally; do not tie the leaves in clumps. Where bulbs are naturalised in grass, do not mow the grass until at least six weeks after the flowers have faded. Premature removal of leaves will have a detrimental effect on growth and flowering the following season.

If drainage is good, bulbs may be left in the ground and clumps can be divided after flowering every three years or so. Bulbs grown indoors in pots can be planted out in the garden after flowering, where they should recover in a season or two.

NARCISSUS AT A GLANCE

Well-known spring-flowering bulbs in a wide variety of flower forms and sizes. Most types are very hardy.

Month	Activity		RECOMMENDED VARIETIES
JAN	flowering	✿	'Carlton'
FEB	flowering	✿	'Cheerfulness'
MAR	flowering	✿	'February Gold'
APR	flowering	✿	'Irene Copeland'
MAY	flowering	✿	'King Alfred'
JUN	/		'Minnow'
JULY	/		'Peeping Tom'
AUG	plant	⚘	'Pipit'
SEPT	plant	⚘	'Thalia'
OCT	plant	⚘	*N. bulbocodium*
NOV	/		*N. canaliculatus*
DEC	/		

NERINE
Nerine, Guernsey lily

THE GUERNSEY LILY, Nerine sarniensis, *needs to be grown in a conservatory or greenhouse except in very mild areas.*

TALL AND ELEGANT, *these bright pink nerines appear as the summer garden fades away in autumn.*

FEATURES

Nerine bowdenii brightens the autumn garden, producing its heads of bright pink flowers before the leaves appear. It is easy to grow and flowers last well when cut. Bulbs should be planted where they can be left undisturbed for several years; they flower best when crowded and after a dry summer. They can also be grown in containers. Flower stems grow 30–45cm (12–18in) high and the deep green, strappy leaves from 20–30cm (8–12in) long. The Guernsey lily (*N. sarniensis*) has bright red flowers, and other species and cultivars of nerines may be red, white, pink or apricot, but only *N. bowdenii* is hardy enough to grow outdoors in this country.

NERINE AT A GLANCE

Heads of funnel-shaped pink flowers appear on leafless stalks in autumn. Needs a warm, sheltered position.

JAN	/	
FEB	sow	🌱
MAR	sow	🌱
APR	plant	🌱
MAY	/	
JUN	/	
JULY	/	
AUG	plant	🌱
SEPT	flowering	🌺
OCT	flowering	🌺
NOV	flowering	🌺
DEC	/	

RECOMMENDED VARIETIES

Nerine bowdenii alba
Nerine bowdenii:
 'Mark Fenwick'
 'Pink Triumph'
 'Wellsii'

N. 'Corusca Major'
N. 'Fothergillii Major'
N. *undulata*

CONDITIONS

Aspect Nerines require full sun and a warm, sheltered spot.
Site A useful plant for borders, especially under the shelter of a south-facing wall. The soil should be free-draining and moderately fertile. In cold areas and with the more tender species, grow bulbs in pots of John Innes potting compost.

GROWING METHOD

Planting Plant in middle to late summer or in mid-spring, 10cm (4in) deep and 15cm (6in) apart. In containers, plant with the neck of the bulb at or just below soil level.
Feeding Can be grown successfully without supplementary fertiliser. However, if you wish, you can give weak liquid fertiliser every couple of weeks once flower buds appear until growth slows down. Water regularly while in active growth but keep the bulbs dry during the dormant period.
Problems No specific problems are known.

FLOWERING

Season Flowers appear during early autumn.
Cutting Nerines last well as cut flowers with frequent water changes.

AFTER FLOWERING

Requirements Cut off spent flower stems. Outdoors, mulch the planting site for winter protection.

ORNITHOGALUM
Chincherinchee, star of Bethlehem

CHINCHERINCHEE *gives a long and pretty floral display, as the flowers open slowly from the bottom up to the top of the cone.*

A BILLOWING CLOUD *of white flowers makes this mass planting a striking feature. Close inspection reveals the pretty green centres.*

FEATURES

There are around 100 species of *Ornithogalum* originating in Africa, Asia and parts of Europe, but the chincherinchee, *O. thyrsoides*, is perhaps the best known, with its imposing spikes of white summer flowers growing up to 45cm (18in). The leaves are narrow and sword-shaped. Other commonly grown species are *O. arabicum*, whose scented white flowers have a striking black eye, *O. nutans*, with delicate spikes of dangling white flowers, and *O. umbellatum*, or star of Bethlehem, which forms clumps of grassy foliage studded with pure white, upward-facing white blooms: these are all spring flowering. Chincherinchee and *O. arabicum* are frost tender.

ORNITHOGALUM AT A GLANCE

Half-hardy and hardy bulbs producing attractive white flowers in spring or early summer.

		RECOMMENDED SPECIES
JAN	/	
FEB	/	*Ornithogalum arabicum*
MAR	/	*O. longibracteatum*
APR	plant ✤/ flower ✤	*O. montanum*
MAY	flowering ✤	*O. nutans*
JUN	flowering ✤	*O. oligophyllum*
JULY	flowering ✤	*O. thyrsoides*
AUG	/	*O. umbellatum*
SEPT	/	
OCT	plant ✤	
NOV	/	
DEC	/	

CONDITIONS

Aspect Prefers an open position in full sun but will grow in light shade. *O. thyrsoides* can be grown outside in summer though it will not survive the winter; in cold areas it can be grown as a pot plant in the home or greenhouse.

Site Good for mixed borders, rockeries or naturalising in grass. The bulbs need well-drained but not very rich soil.

GROWING METHOD

Planting Plant bulbs in spring or autumn, 5cm (2in) deep and about 20–30cm (8–12in) apart.

Feeding Not usually essential, but an application of balanced or high potash fertiliser given as the plants start into growth may improve flowering. Watering is not necessary unless the season is exceptionally dry; for container-grown plants, keep the compost just moist.

Problems This bulb is generally trouble-free.

FLOWERING

Season Flowers will appear spring and early summer.

Cutting This is a first class cut flower.

AFTER FLOWERING

Requirements Cut spent flower stems at ground level. Non-hardy species should be lifted in autumn and stored in a dry, cool place for replanting the following spring. Hardy species can be divided after flowering and replanted immediately.

OXALIS
Wood sorrel

THE SATINY WHITE FLOWERS on Oxalis purpurea *'Alba' are a far cry from the weedy forms of oxalis that invade our gardens.*

THIS PRETTY PINK OXALIS makes a charming groundcover here on the edge of a paved area.

FEATURES

A number of species of oxalis are very invasive, but others are very decorative and well worth growing. Most have clover-like leaves and five-petalled, satiny flowers which are furled in bud. The usual colour is pink or white; there are also purple, yellow, orange or red varieties. Some species need greenhouse cultivation in this country. Height varies from 5–20cm (2–8in). *O. adenophylla* is the most popular species, with greyish leaves and silvery flowers; *O. enneaphylla* has white flowers and attractive, folded, silvery leaves. *O. laciniata* has narrow leaflets and purple, veined flowers. Once known as *O. deppei*, *O. tetraphylla* has brown-marked leaves and pink flowers.

CONDITIONS

Aspect	Grow in full sun for good flowering and compact leaf growth.
Site	Grow on a rockery or near the front of a border, preferably in a confined bed where growth can be controlled. The more invasive varieties are best grown in pots. Free-draining soil is preferred.

GROWING METHOD

Planting	Plant in early autumn, 7.5cm (3in) deep and 10cm (4in) apart. It is usual to plant clumps in growth rather than the tiny tubers or rhizomes.
Feeding	Supplementary fertiliser is rarely needed.
Problems	Few problems are usually encountered although some oxalis do suffer from the fungal leaf disease rust. Pick off the worst affected leaves and avoid overhead watering.

FLOWERING

Season	Most species flower through early and mid-summer.
Cutting	Flowers are unsuitable for cutting.

AFTER FLOWERING

Requirements	Plants can be divided after flowering in summer. Clear away dead foliage once the leaves have died down; beware of putting plant debris from invasive varieties on the compost heap.

OXALIS AT A GLANCE

A low-growing, clump-forming plant with clover-like leaves and attractive, satiny flowers. Can be invasive.

		RECOMMENDED VARIETIES
JAN	/	
FEB	/	'Beatrice Anderson'
MAR	/	'Bowles' White'
APR	/	'Ione Hecker'
MAY	/	'Royal Velvet'
JUN	flowering	
JULY	flowering	*O. enneaphylla:*
AUG	/	'Alba'
SEPT	planting	'Minutifolia'
OCT	planting	'Rosea'
NOV	/	
DEC	/	*O. tetraphylla:*
		'Iron Cross'

POLIANTHES TUBEROSA
Tuberose

'THE PEARL', a double-flowered cultivar, is the variety most often available to home gardeners.

PINK-TINGED BUDS open to the heavy-textured cream flowers, so prized for their characteristic strong perfume.

FEATURES

Tuberose is known for its heavily perfumed flowers – tuberose oil is used in perfume production. A double form known as 'The Pearl' is the most widely grown. It can be grown in a sunny, sheltered border, but is often more reliable when grown as a conservatory or house plant, especially in cooler areas. The scent can more easily be appreciated under cover.

A flower spike 60cm (2ft) or more high appears from the basal leaves in summer and early autumn. The waxy flowers have a heavy texture and are white with a pinkish tinge at the base. Tubers that have bloomed once will not reflower the following season – new tubers must be planted each year.

POLIANTHES AT A GLANCE

Valued for its intensely fragrant, creamy white flowers which are carried on tall spikes in late summer.

Month			Recommended Varieties
JAN	/		
FEB	/		*Polianthes tuberosa:*
MAR	plant	👈	'The Pearl'
APR	/		
MAY	/		
JUN	/		
JULY	/		
AUG	flowering	🌿	
SEPT	flowering	🌿	
OCT	flowering	🌿	
NOV	/		
DEC	/		

CONDITIONS

Aspect Prefers full sun and shelter from strong wind.

Site Grow in a warm, sheltered border, or in containers for the conservatory, house or greenhouse. Use either John Innes or soilless potting compost.

GROWING METHOD

Planting Plant 5cm (2in) deep, or 2.5cm (1in) deep in containers.

Feeding Once growth appears, liquid feed with a balanced fertiliser every 14 days through the growing season. Water sparingly to start with, but keep the plant moist at all times when in growth.

Problems No particular problems are known.

FLOWERING

Season Flowers should appear during late summer or in early autumn.

Cutting Makes an excellent cut flower. Cut spikes for the vase when two or three of the lower blooms are fully open. Removing spent flowers from the spike as they fade will help to prolong the vase life.

AFTER FLOWERING

Requirements Tubers are usually discarded at the end of the season. Offsets are produced, and these may sometimes be grown on to flower in two years or so, but they are often disappointing.

RANUNCULUS ASIATICUS

Ranunculus, Persian buttercup

TAFFETA-LIKE PETALS are ruffled and folded closely together around the dark eye of this vibrant scarlet ranunculus.

RANUNCULUS FLOWERS last well in a sheltered, sunny garden and close planting will produce a wonderfully colourful display.

FEATURES

One of the brightest and most colourful of all spring-flowering bulbs, ranunculus can be massed in mixed colours or blocks of single colour in the garden or in containers. Left in the ground they may give several seasons, although they are often treated as annuals. However, the woody, oddly shaped tubers can be lifted and stored like other bulbs.

The many-petalled flowers of ranunculus come in bright yellow, cream, white, reds and pinks, and stems of some strains may reach 45cm (18in) in height. Although there are single flowered varieties, double or semi-double types are by far the most popular. They are usually sold as colour mixtures, but separate red and yellow forms are sometimes available from specialist suppliers.

Ranunculus blooms make very good cut flowers, lasting well in the vase.

RANUNCULUS AT A GLANCE

Brightly coloured, many-petalled, poppy-like flowers are carried above attractive ferny foliage in summer.

		RECOMMENDED VARIETIES
JAN	/	
FEB	/	'Red form'
MAR	planting	'Yellow form'
APR	planting	'Accolade'
MAY	/	
JUN	flowering	
JULY	flowering	
AUG	flowering	
SEPT	/	
OCT	/	
NOV	/	
DEC	/	

CONDITIONS

Aspect   Prefers full sun all day with shelter from very strong wind.

Site   Ideal for beds, borders and containers, where they will make a colourful display. The soil should be well drained, ideally with plenty of compost or manure dug in a month or so before planting.

GROWING METHOD

Planting   Plant the woody, tuberous roots 3–5cm (1–2in) deep and about 15cm (6in) apart, with the claws pointing down, in early spring. Soaking the tubers in water for a few hours before planting gets them off to a good start.

Feeding   Liquid feed with a balanced fertiliser every two weeks from when the flower buds start to appear. Keep the soil moist once the ferny leaves appear, particularly during bud formation and flowering.

Problems   Usually trouble free, though powdery mildew may occur in hot, dry seasons. Spray with a general fungicide if necessary.

FLOWERING

Season   Flowers throughout the summer.

Cutting   Cut flowers early in the morning and change the water frequently to prolong vase life.

AFTER FLOWERING

Requirements   Cut off spent flower stems. When the foliage has died down completely, tubers can be lifted, cleaned and stored in dry peat in a frost-free place until the following spring. After three seasons tubers are best replaced.

RHODOHYPOXIS BAURII
Rose grass

TINY MAGENTA CENTRES *emphasise the stark white of this pretty rose grass. The unusual flower form is clearly seen here.*

DEEP ROSE-PINK *in colour, this form of rose grass is sometimes sold as 'Rosy Posy'. It gives a long flowering display.*

FEATURES

This enchanting little plant, which comes from high altitude areas of South Africa, is ideally suited to growing in a rock garden, on the edge of a border or in pots. The slightly hairy leaves, similar to those of a broad-leaf grass, grow to around 10cm (4in) high. The flowers, which are white or pink through to deep rosy crimson, are about the same height. As they have become better known several varieties with deeper colour or larger flowers have become available. They have six petals with one set of three appearing to be set on top of the other, so the flower has no visible eye. The floral display is long lasting, from late spring through to late summer.

If grown in the garden the positions of these plants should be marked in some way as they are completely dormant during winter.

RHODOHYPOXIS AT A GLANCE

A tuberous alpine with mounds of attractive pink or white flowers carried for a very long season.

		RECOMMENDED VARIETIES
JAN	/	
FEB	/	'Alba'
MAR	plant	'Dulcie'
APR	plant	'Dawn'
MAY	flowering	'Douglas'
JUN	flowering	'Eva-Kate'
JULY	flowering	'Fred Broome'
AUG	flowering	'Garnett'
SEPT	flowering	'Harlequin'
OCT	/	'Picta'
NOV	/	'Ruth'
DEC	/	'Stella'

CONDITIONS

Aspect Grows best in full sun in a sheltered spot.
Site Suitable for rockeries, scree gardens or containers. The soil must be well drained but enriched with decayed organic matter. It needs to be lime free, as rose grass is not tolerant of alkaline soils. Good quality potting compost mixed with a little extra sharp sand should be adequate for containers.

GROWING METHOD

Planting Tubers should be planted in late spring about 5cm (2in) deep and 10cm (4in) apart. Lift and divide offsets in autumn.
Feeding Mulch garden plants with decayed manure or compost in late winter or early spring. Potted plants that have not been repotted will benefit from slow-release fertiliser in early spring. Water regularly during the growing period in dry spells, but keep dry through winter.
Problems No specific problems are known.

FLOWERING

Season The long flowering period runs from late spring through to late summer.
Cutting Flowers are unsuitable for picking.

AFTER FLOWERING

Requirements Spent blooms can be snipped off or ignored. Protect plants from excess winter rainfall; a sheet of glass supported horizontally over the plants on four wooden stakes should prevent the crowns rotting off in wet weather.

ROMULEA
Romulea

THE CHARMING FLOWERS of little Romulea rosea *may be best appreciated when it is grown in a container.*

PALE LAVENDER PETALS and a recessed deep gold throat make Romulea bulbocodium *worth growing. It tolerates cool conditions.*

FEATURES

These small plants have grassy leaves and brightly coloured, crocus-like flowers. There are 75 species native to parts of Africa, the Mediterranean and Europe, most in cultivation being South African.

Growing 7.5–15cm (3–6in) high, depending on species, they are ideal for rock gardens and pots where their neat growth can be admired. The colour range includes cream and yellow, many shades of blue and violet and also pinks and reds: many flowers have a very attractive 'eye' of contrasting colour in the centre of the flower. The most popular type, *R. bulbocodium*, has pale lavender flowers with a yellow throat, and is hardier than some of the other species. Flowers remain closed in dull weather.

ROMULEA AT A GLANCE

A low-growing plant with crocus-like flowers which open wide in full sun. Needs a protected position.

JAN	/	
FEB	/	
MAR	flowering	**RECOMMENDED SPECIES**
APR	flowering	*Romulea bulbocodium clusiana*
MAY	flowering	*Romulea flava*
JUN	/	*Romulea sabulosa*
JULY	/	
AUG	/	
SEPT	plant	
OCT	plant	
NOV	/	
DEC	/	

CONDITIONS

Aspect Needs full sun all day. The flowers will not open in shady conditions.

Site Grows best when grown in a sharply draining, rather sandy soil. Good for scree beds, rockeries and containers.

GROWING METHOD

Planting The small corms should be planted some 5cm (2in) deep and 5–7.5cm (2–3in) apart in autumn.

Feeding Feeding is not normally necessary for this plant, but in poor soils some balanced fertiliser may be applied as growth begins. Water freely to keep the soil moist through the growing season but keep plants dry during the summer, when they die down.

Problems No specific pest or disease problems are known for romulea.

FLOWERING

Season Flowers are carried throughout the spring months.

Cutting None of the species has flowers that are suitable for cutting.

AFTER FLOWERING

Requirements Protect the crowns with a mulch of peat or similar material for the winter months. Overcrowded clumps can be lifted and divided when the flowers have faded.

SCHIZOSTYLIS COCCINEA
Kaffir lily

THE EXTENDED FLOWER *spikes give the appearance of a small gladiolus, thought the individual flowers are more delicate.*

THE RICH ROSE *flowers of* Schizostylis *'Tambara' are displayed to great effect against evergreen shrubs in the late autumn garden.*

FEATURES

The lovely, scarlet or pink, gladiolus-like flowers of schizostylis add a very welcome splash of colour to autumn borders, coming as they do right at the end of the season. The tall, grassy leaves form a clump from which 60–90cm (2–3ft) spikes of flowers arise, bearing some 8–10 open, star-shaped blooms. There are several named varieties in a range of pink and red shades: 'Major' has large, deep red flowers, 'Viscountess Byng' is a delicate pink, and 'Tambara' is a rich, rosy pink. 'November Cheer' is one of the latest-flowering varieties.
Schizostylis is not suitable for cold, exposed gardens, but grows and spreads rapidly where conditions suit it.

SCHIZOSTYLIS AT A GLANCE

A valuable late autumn-flowering plant for the border, with colourful scarlet or pink, gladiolus-like flower spikes.

JAN	/	
FEB	/	
MAR	plant 🖐	**RECOMMENDED VARIETIES**
APR	plant 🖐	'Jennifer'
MAY	/	'Mrs Hegarty'
JUN	/	'November Cheer'
JULY	/	'Sunrise'
AUG	/	'Tambara'
SEPT	flowering 🌼	'Viscountess Byng'
OCT	flowering 🌼	
NOV	flowering 🌼	
DEC	/	

CONDITIONS

Aspect   A sheltered spot in full sun or light shade suits this plant.
Site   Suitable for the middle of the flower border; in cold districts they do well as pot plants in a conservatory or greenhouse. Moisture-retentive, fertile soil is required.

GROWING METHOD

Planting   Plant in spring, 5cm (2in) deep and 30cm (12in) apart. Pot-grown plants are available for planting in summer and autumn. Rhizomes can also be planted in 20cm (8in) pots of soilless or John Innes compost in a sheltered position outdoors, being brought into a cool conservatory or greenhouse before the first frosts for flowering inside.
Feeding   Keep the soil moist at all times. Feed pot-grown plants with high potash liquid fertiliser every 14 days from early summer until flower buds form.
Problems   No specific problems are generally experienced.

FLOWERING

Season   Flowers from late September into November.
Cutting   The flower spikes are excellent for cutting, lasting well in water. Pick them when the buds start to show colour.

AFTER FLOWERING

Requirements Cut down faded flower stems. Protect the crowns with a mulch of chipped bark, straw or dry leaves over winter. Overcrowded plants can be divided in autumn.

SCILLA
Squill

A STARBURST of bright blue flowers topped with golden stamens makes up the pretty inflorescence of Scilla peruviana, *the Cuban lily.*

THE SIBERIAN SQUILL, Scilla siberica, *makes its appearance in early spring. 'Atrocoerulea' has particularly rich blue flowers.*

FEATURES

The most familiar scillas are the dwarf varieties that flower in early spring. They include *Scilla siberica* (Siberian squill), which has clusters of nodding blue bells about 15cm (6in) high, and *Scilla mischtschenkoana* (*S. tubergeniana*), which has starry, pale blue flowers with a deeper blue stripe on the petals. This species grows only 5–10cm (2–4in) high. *S. bifolia* grows 5–15cm (2–6in), with a spike of 15 or more star-shaped flowers in blue, pink or white. Leaves of all these species are elongated and strap shaped. *Scilla peruviana*, the Cuban lily, is quite different – a tall, early summer-flowering bulb with densely packed, conical heads of purple-blue flowers.

SCILLA AT A GLANCE

Mainly dwarf bulbs with starry or bell-shaped blue or white flowers in early spring.

JAN	/	
FEB	flowering	🌱
MAR	flowering	🌱
APR	flowering	🌱
MAY	flowering	🌱
JUN	flowering	🌱
JULY	/	
AUG	plant	🌿
SEPT	plant	🌿
OCT	plant	🌿
NOV	/	
DEC	/	

RECOMMENDED VARIETIES

Scilla bifolia:
'Rosea'
Scilla siberica:
'Alba'
'Spring Beauty'
Scilla peruviana:
'Alba'
Scilla peruviana elegans
S. p. venusta

CONDITIONS

Aspect Tolerates full sun but the flowers will have better, longer lasting colour if they are grown in semi-shade.

Site Grow in beds and borders, in almost any kind of soil as long as it drains well. Soils enriched with organic matter will give better results.

GROWING METHOD

Planting Plant the bulbs about 5–10cm (2–4in) deep and 15–20cm (6–8in) apart in late summer or early autumn.

Feeding Apply a balanced fertiliser after flowering in early summer. Water during dry spells before and during the flowering season.

Problems No specific pest or disease problems are known for this plant.

FLOWERING

Season The flower spikes appear during late spring and early summer.

Cutting Flowers can be cut successfully for indoor decoration.

AFTER FLOWERING

Requirements Faded flower spikes should be cut off just above ground level. Clumps will usually need to be lifted only every 4–5 years unless they are very congested. Divide crowded clumps in late summer, replanting immediately to avoid drying out of the bulbs.

SINNINGIA
Gloxinia

THE VELVETY texture of trumpet-shaped gloxinia flowers shows up well here on the variety 'Blanche de Meru'.

'GREGOR MENDEL' is one of several fully double-flowered varieties. The heavy heads of bloom may need supporting with thin canes.

FEATURES

Gloxinias are tender plants suitable for growing in the home, greenhouse or conservatory, where they will make an impressive, colourful display. The large, showy, brilliantly coloured flowers are trumpet shaped, often with speckled throats. Both flowers and leaves have a velvety feel and appearance: the large leaves are mid-green and oval.

Flowers are produced in abundance on well-grown plants, and are available in many colours, from white through pink and red to deepest blue and violet. The edges of the petals may be ruffled, or frilled with a contrasting colour; there are several double-flowered varieties.

SINNINGIA AT A GLANCE

A showy house plant with colourful, velvety-textured flowers. Minimum temperature 15ºC (60ºF).

JAN	plant 🌱	**RECOMMENDED VARIETIES**
FEB	plant 🌱	
MAR	plant 🌱	'Blanche de Meru'
APR	/	'Mont Blanc'
MAY	/	'Princess Elizabeth'
JUN	flowering 🍂	'Gregor Mendel'
JULY	flowering 🍂	
AUG	flowering 🍂	
SEPT	/	
OCT	/	
NOV	/	
DEC	/	

CONDITIONS

Aspect   Choose a bright position, but not one which is in direct sun or the foliage will be scorched.

Site   Gloxinias are house plants requiring average warmth; they dislike hot, dry air and benefit from standing on a dish of moist pebbles for increased humidity. Moisture-retentive soilless potting compost should be used.

GROWING METHOD

Planting   Start the tubers off in moist peat or compost in a frost-free position in spring, potting them up individually once the shoots start to grow. Tubers must be planted with the dished side up, level with the surface of the compost – not buried.

Feeding   Apply high potash liquid fertiliser every 14 days during the growing season. Keep the compost only just moist until growth has started, then water more freely. Take care to keep water splashes off the leaves and flowers, and never waterlog the compost.

Problems   Hot, dry air causes the leaves to shrivel and flower buds to fall before opening. Overwatering leads to rotting of the roots.

FLOWERING

Season   Flowers throughout the summer.
Cutting   Not suitable for cutting

AFTER FLOWERING

Requirements Gradually reduce watering until the leaves have died back, then store the tubers in dry compost in a cool but frost-free place. Repot in fresh potting compost in spring.

SPARAXIS TRICOLOR
Harlequin flower

HARLEQUIN FLOWERS come in a veritable kaleidoscope of colours, with the patterned throat revealing yet more colours and patterns.

THE STRONG, BRIGHT COLOURS of harlequin flowers are shown to best advantage when they are planted in an open, sunny spot.

FEATURES

This showy, easy-care plant has bright flowers of yellow, red, pink, orange or purple carried on stems that can be anywhere from 15–45cm (6–18in) high. Many of the brightly coloured flowers have a darker purple or deep red area in the centre and a yellow throat. Harlequin flowers hybridise readily, often producing seedlings that have interesting colour variations. These are bulbs that thrive in dry, warm areas of the garden. They look their best when mass planted but can also be grown in containers, where they should be crowded together for best effect. The flowers cut well for indoor decoration. Harlequin flower bulbs increase rapidly by offsets.

SPARAXIS AT A GLANCE

Very brightly coloured, star-shaped flowers are carried on slender stems in early summer. Not suitable for cold, exposed gardens.

		RECOMMENDED VARIETIES
JAN	/	
FEB	/	Usually supplied as a
MAR	/	colour mixture
APR	/	
MAY	flowering	
JUN	flowering	
JULY	/	
AUG	/	
SEPT	/	
OCT	/	
NOV	plant	
DEC	/	

CONDITIONS

Aspect Needs full sun all day for best results.
Site Sparaxis needs a sheltered spot in a reasonably mild area to do well; in cold gardens it is best grown in containers under cover. Soil must be well-drained and moderately fertile.

GROWING METHOD

Planting Corms should be planted 7.5cm (3in) deep and 7.5–10cm (3–4in) apart in mid-autumn. Mulch the planting area with chipped bark or leafmould for winter protection.
Feeding In very poor soil apply a balanced fertiliser in early summer after flowering. Mulch the soil in late winter with well-rotted organic matter. In dry seasons, water when the foliage emerges and as buds and flowers develop if necessary.
Problems No specific problems are known.

FLOWERING

Season Flowering should be abundant in late spring and early summer.
Cutting Sparaxis makes a good cut flower for the home and should last well in water.

AFTER FLOWERING

Requirements Allow foliage to die down naturally, then lift the corms and dry them off until it is time to replant in autumn. Any cormlets that have formed can be removed when the corms are lifted and replanted separately.

SPREKELIA FORMOSISSIMA
Jacobean lily

THE SCULPTURED LINES of Jacobean lilies need to be appreciated at close quarters. Growing them in containers is a perfect solution.

THE DARK CRIMSON of the flowers tends to recede into the deep green foliage but still gives a lovely rich glow.

FEATURES

The rich crimson flowers of Jacobean lily are carried singly on stems 30–45cm (12–18in) high and the foliage, which is about the same height, appears with or just before the flowers. This plant is sometimes called the Aztec lily and is in fact native to Mexico where it occurs in open, sunny places, often in poor soil. The unusual shape of the flower gives rise to another common name, orchid amaryllis, and the exotic-looking flower could easily be mistaken for an orchid. Unfortunately it is suitable for gardens in mild areas only; in less favoured climates it must be grown as a greenhouse or conservatory plant. Formerly much more widely grown than it is today, it deserves to become more popular.

SPREKELIA AT A GLANCE

An exotic-looking, rather tender plant which needs greenhouse conditions in cooler areas. Minimum temperature 10°C (45°F).

		RECOMMENDED VARIETIES
JAN	/	Only the straight species is grown – no cultivars or varieties of this plant are available.
FEB	/	
MAR	/	
APR	plant 🖐	
MAY	/	
JUN	flowering 🌿	
JULY	/	
AUG	/	
SEPT	/	
OCT	/	
NOV	/	
DEC	/	

CONDITIONS

Aspect   Grows best in full sun with wind protection. Indoors it likes a bright position.

Site   Suitable for a sheltered border in mild areas, or containers in a greenhouse or conservatory. Outdoors, soil must be well drained and enriched with compost or manure. Use John Innes potting compost for containers.

GROWING METHOD

Planting   Plant bulbs in spring, 5cm (2in) deep and 20cm (8in) apart. In containers, plant with the neck of the bulb just above the compost surface.

Feeding   Give a high potash liquid feed every two or three weeks throughout the growing season. Water container plants regularly until the foliage starts to die down.

Problems   No specific problems are known.

FLOWERING

Season   The showy flowers appear in early summer.

Cutting   Can be cut for the vase but usually better enjoyed on the plant.

AFTER FLOWERING

Requirements   When the leaves die down, lift outdoor bulbs and keep them in a cool, dry place. For container-grown plants, allow the compost to dry out when the leaves die down, then keep the bulb dry in its pot until spring when watering will start it into growth again.

STERNBERGIA LUTEA
Autumn daffodil, lily-of-the-field

MOST SCHOLARS today believe Sternbergia lutea *is the plant referred to in the Bible as 'the lily of the field'.*

SHORT IN STATURE but big on impact, lily-of-the-field is one of the most delightful of bulbs, especially so as it blooms in autumn.

FEATURES

Clear, bright yellow flowers, rather like crocuses, appear on 15cm (6in) stems from their surround of shorter, dark green, strappy leaves. The foliage persists until spring when it dies down to remain dormant until the following autumn. Ideal for the rock garden, these plants also show to advantage when planted in the garden in good-sized groups where they can be left to multiply. This is a bulb that could be naturalised in turf but the area would have to be well marked to avoid cutting off the emerging growth in autumn, and the grass could not be mown for several months. Lily-of-the-field can be grown in containers but they are more successful in the open ground.

STERNBERGIA AT A GLANCE

A crocus-like bulb with flowers appearing in late summer and autumn. Needs very well-drained soil to thrive.

		RECOMMENDED VARIETIES
JAN	/	
FEB	/	*Sternbergia lutea:*
MAR	/	Angustifolia Group
APR	/	
MAY	/	*Sternbergia clusiana*
JUN	/	
JULY	plant 🖐	*Sternbergia sicula*
AUG	plant 🖐	
SEPT	flowering 🌼	
OCT	flowering 🌼	
NOV	/	
DEC	/	

CONDITIONS

Aspect   Prefers full sun: a summer baking of the dormant bulbs is necessary for good flowering in the autumn.

Site   Suitable for a rockery, raised bed, or a sunny, reasonably sheltered border. Very well-drained soil is essential for this plant. Well-rotted organic matter can be dug into the bed ahead of planting.

GROWING METHOD

Planting   Plant bulbs in summer about 12.5cm (5in) deep and the same distance apart.

Feeding   Supplementary fertiliser is generally not needed.

Problems   The main problem encountered is rotting of bulbs due to heavy or poorly drained soil. Improve drainage by incorporating sharp sand into the planting area.

FLOWERING

Season   The small, bright golden flowers appear in autumn.

Cutting   These flowers are not suitable for cutting.

AFTER FLOWERING

Requirements   Ensure the plants are allowed to remain dry once the foliage has died down in early summer. The site may need protection from excessive summer rain with a cloche or similar. Do not disturb established plants unless it is essential.

TIGRIDIA PAVONIA
Tiger flower, peacock flower

THE SHOWY FLOWERS of Tigridia pavonia *often have colourful spotting in the centre, making it worth studying them closely.*

EACH EXOTIC bloom lasts only a day, but is swiftly followed by others to give a succession of flowers over several weeks.

FEATURES

Although each flower of the tiger or peacock flower lasts only a day, there is a succession of spectacular blooms over a long period. Flowers have six petals; the outer petals are large and broad, the inner ones smaller and thinner, usually spotted with a contrasting colour. The species is red with a spotted yellow and purple centre but there is a large range of colours available, in combinations of white, cream, yellow, orange, pink, mauve and red, with contrasting spotting around the centre of each flower. The tiger flower is also called jockey's cap lily in some parts of the world. Plants usually grow to around 45cm (18in). They are often included in mixed borders of summer-flowering shrubs and perennials.

TIGRIDIA AT A GLANCE

Spectacularly colourful but short-lived flowers are produced in succession from mid to late summer. Best in warmer areas.

JAN	/	RECOMMENDED VARIETIES
FEB	/	
MAR	/	Generally available only as colour mixtures.
APR	plant	
MAY	plant	
JUN	/	
JULY	/	
AUG	flowering	
SEPT	flowering	
OCT	/	
NOV	/	
DEC	/	

CONDITIONS

Aspect Prefers full sun with some wind protection. Grows best in warm, sheltered gardens.

Site Grow the plants towards the front of beds and borders, where their flamoyant flowers can be appreciated close at hand. They need well-drained but not particularly rich soil.

GROWING METHOD

Planting Plant in mid to late spring 10cm (4in) deep and about 15–20cm (6–8in) apart.

Feeding Growth is usually improved by the application of a balanced fertiliser in spring. Occasional liquid feeds of a high potash fertiliser can be given through the growing season. Water during spring and summer in dry spells.

Problems No specific problems are usually experienced with this plant.

FLOWERING

Season Blooms appear from middle to late summer into the early autumn.

Cutting Flowers are not suitable for cutting.

AFTER FLOWERING

Requirements Remove spent flower stems. In sheltered, mild areas and in free-draining soil the bulbs can be left in the ground over winter, but more reliable results are obtained by lifting before the first frosts, and storing bulbs in a frost-free place until the following spring.

TRILLIUM
Wake robin, wood lily

THE LATIN NAME *Trillium* refers to 'three' and wake robin has everything in threes: three petals, three sepals and a ring of three leaves.

THE LITTLE FLOWERS of wake robin will make a delightful sight as they light up a shaded part of the garden.

FEATURES

Trillium grandiflorum is a charming woodland plant which hails from North America. With its three pure white petals and dark foliage, it is a most arresting sight when naturalised in groups under trees to simulate its native habitat. It is not a difficult plant to grow and is well worth seeking out – it can be vigorous and long lived in the right conditions. The white flowers slowly age to pink and there is an attractive double form available called *T. grandiflorum flore pleno*. Plants grow to 38cm (15in) or so high.

Other species worth growing include *T. sessile*, with dark red flowers springing from bronze blotched foliage; *T. erectum*, with maroon flowers and lighter green foliage, and *T. undulatum*, which has white or pinkish flowers streaked with red.

TRILLIUM AT A GLANCE

Attractive plants for lightly shaded or woodland conditions, with white, three-petalled flowers in early summer.

		RECOMMENDED VARIETIES
JAN	/	
FEB	/	*Trillium grandiflorum*
MAR	/	'Flore Pleno'
APR	flowering	
MAY	flowering	*Trillium erectum albiflorum*
JUN	flowering	
JULY	/	*Trillium erectum luteum*
AUG	plant	
SEPT	plant	*Trillium sessile luteum*
OCT	plant	
NOV	/	
DEC	/	

CONDITIONS

Aspect   Needs light shade at all times or the dappled sunlight provided by overhead trees or shrubs.

Site   An ideal plant for a woodland garden or a shady border. Does best in very rich, moist, but free-draining soil. Copious quantities of well-rotted cow manure or leafmould should be dug into the soil before planting. Mulch well in late winter, too.

GROWING METHOD

Planting   Plant rhizomes 7.5cm (3in) deep in late summer or early autumn. Plant in groups at 30cm (12in) or so intervals.

Feeding   An annual dressing of leafmould or well-rotted manure should provide sufficient nutrients, but an application of general fertiliser can be given in spring. The soil must not dry out in spring and summer and so give careful attention to watering in dry weather.

Problems   Slugs and snails may damage newly emerging leaves or flowers; otherwise it is generally trouble-free.

FLOWERING

Season   Flowers will appear somewhere between mid-spring and early summer.

Cutting   Flowers are not suitable for picking.

AFTER FLOWERING

Requirements   No special attention is needed after flowering apart from tidying dead foliage. Crowded clumps can be divided and replanted immediately in autumn.

TRITELEIA
syn. *Brodiaea laxa*

'QUEEN FABIOLA' is probably the most widely planted of the triteleias. The paler centre gives definition to the flower form.

BLUE FLOWERS are always a favourite, and the violet-blue, starry flowers of these triteleias fill a sheltered pocket in the garden.

FEATURES

These pretty bulbous plants are native to Oregon and California. There is some confusion over their correct name; they are often listed as brodiaea, with some species as dichelostemma. *T. laxa* is the most popular form. Flower stems may be 45–60cm(18–24in) or so high with the strappy leaves growing to about 30cm (12in). The starry flowers are carried in loose clusters and are pale or violet blue with the most popular cultivar, 'Queen Fabiola', producing deeper violet-blue blooms with a pale centre. The foliage dies back in spring while the plant is in bloom, and the corm remains dormant from mid-summer until winter.

TRITELEIA AT A GLANCE

Dainty clusters of tubular blue blooms are carried on slender stems in mid-summer. Well-drained soil is essential.

		RECOMMENDED VARIETIES
JAN	/	
FEB	/	*Triteleia hyacinthina*
MAR	/	
APR	/	*Triteleia ixioides*
MAY	flowering 🌺	
JUN	flowering 🌺	*Triteleia laxa:*
JULY	flowering 🌺	'Queen Fabiola'
AUG	/	
SEPT	plant 🌱	*Triteleia peduncularis*
OCT	/	
NOV	/	
DEC	/	

CONDITIONS

Aspect An open, sunny but sheltered site is necessary.
Site Grow this plant in the flower border or in containers. The soil must be light and very well drained; triteleia cannot stand waterlogging. It can be grown in containers of sandy potting compost where the garden soil is heavy.

GROWING METHOD

Planting Plant corms 7.5–10cm (3–4in) deep and 10–15cm (4–6in) apart in autumn.
Feeding A balanced or high potash fertiliser can be given when the flower buds appear, but normally no feeding is necessary. Plants in containers can be liquid fed fortnightly. Watering is not normally necessary; the soil should be allowed to dry out while the corm is dormant during the summer.
Problems There are no specific pest or disease problems known for this plant.

FLOWERING

Season Flowers appear from early to mid-summer.
Cutting Blooms last particularly well as a cut flower.

AFTER FLOWERING

Requirements Flowering stems can be cut off once they are past their peak, or left to set seed. Plants resent disturbance, so should be left alone once planted.

TRITONIA
Tritonia

THIS ORANGE TRITONIA (Tritonia crocata) *is planted beside a path where it revels in the reflected heat and somewhat dry conditions. Like most tritonias, it will increase rapidly if it is happy with the growing conditions.*

FEATURES

This is a most undemanding little plant that will give great value in containers or as a cut flower. Tritonias are not fully hardy and in colder areas need to be grown indoors, but in sheltered gardens in milder parts of the country they can be grown outside successfully as long as they have full sun and a well-drained soil.

Most species flower from middle to late spring or in early summer on spikes that are around 30cm (12in) high. *T. crocata* usually has bright orange flowers with darker markings in the throat but there are other forms with bright pink, salmon or scarlet flowers. *T. disticha rubrolucens* has rose pink flowers and is hardier; it is often listed as *T. rosea*.

TRITONIA AT A GLANCE

Colourful, freesia-like flowers in late spring and early summer. Not suitable for growing outdoors in colder areas.

		RECOMMENDED VARIETIES
JAN	/	Usually available only as colour mixtures.
FEB	/	
MAR	/	
APR	/	
MAY	flowering 🌸	
JUN	flowering 🌸	
JULY	/	
AUG	/	
SEPT	plant ✍	
OCT	/	
NOV	/	
DEC	/	

CONDITIONS

Aspect   Grows best in full sun, preferably with shelter from strong wind.

Site   In mild areas, tritonias do well in pockets of a rockery or planted in generous clumps in a garden bed. Soil must be well drained but it need not be very rich. In cold gardens, grow the corms in pots of John Innes or soilless potting compost.

GROWING METHOD

Planting   Plant the corms about 5cm (2in) deep and 10–15cm (4–6in) apart in autumn. Five corms can be grown in a 15cm (6in) pot.

Feeding   A light application of balanced fertiliser can be given as growth starts. In containers, liquid feed every 14–21 days. Begin watering container plants when the leaves appear but allow the compost to dry out once the leaves start to turn yellow.

Problems   No specific problems are known.

FLOWERING

Season   Flowers are carried from mid-spring to early summer.

Cutting   Flowers will last in the vase for up to a week.

AFTER FLOWERING

Requirements   Cut off spent flower stems. Mulch plants growing outdoors for winter protection: allow container plants to remain dry in their pots until planting time.

TULBAGHIA VIOLACEA
Wild garlic

THE PALE PURPLE flowers of wild garlic are pleasantly fragrant, though the crushed foliage has a distinctive onion smell.

THE FLOWERS APPEAR throughout the summer above the clumps of vigorous, grey-green foliage.

FEATURES

This is another plant which needs warm, sheltered gardens to do well when left outdoors, though it can be grown as a container plant very successfully in cooler areas. The strappy leaves grow to about 30cm (12in) with the flowering stems standing 10cm (4in) or more above the foliage. The individual rosy-violet flowers form a rounded head of bloom. Society garlic flowers through the summer, and stems can be cut for the vase. *Tulbaghia natalensis* grows to 15cm (6in) high and has fragrant white flowers with a yellow centre that gives them a narcissus-like appearance. This is a hardier species which is usually more successful in colder gardens, though it is not as common as *T. violacea*.

TULBAGHIA AT A GLANCE

A slightly tender plant with mounds of grassy foliage and heads of pretty pink summer flowers.

		RECOMMENDED VARIETIES
JAN	/	
FEB	/	*Tulbaghia violacea pallida*
MAR	/	
APR	plant 🖐	*Tulbaghia violacea:*
MAY	/	'Silver Lace'
JUN	flowering 🌿	
JULY	flowering 🌿	
AUG	flowering 🌿	
SEPT	/	
OCT	/	
NOV	/	
DEC	/	

CONDITIONS

Aspect Prefers a position in full sun.
Site Tulbaghia is a good plant for seaside gardens, and can be included in a mixed border of annuals and perennials or grown in containers. Soil should be well drained and contain plenty of well-rotted organic matter.

GROWING METHOD

Planting Plant in spring about 2.5cm (1in) deep and 20cm (8in) or so apart. Congested clumps can be lifted and divided in spring.
Feeding If the organic content of the soil is high little extra feeding is needed. However, a light dressing of balanced fertiliser may be given as growth becomes active. Keep the soil moist during the growing season, watering in dry spells as necessary.
Problems No specific problems are known.

FLOWERING

Season Flowers are carried all through summer.
Cutting Flowers are very decorative when cut for the vase, although the smell of the foliage may discourage some people.

AFTER FLOWERING

Requirements Tidy up the foliage and apply a mulch of chipped bark, leafmould or dry leaves for winter protection. Container plants should be allowed to dry out and moved under cover for the winter.

THE BIZARRE FORM of parrot tulips is exemplified by this dark crimson flower. People either love these forms or hate them.

THE BURGUNDY of these full-blown tulips will appeal to lovers of the unusual but they may be hard to incorporate into the garden scheme.

continued from page 101

CONDITIONS

Aspect   Tulips need full sun for at least half the day, with some wind protection.

Site   Grow tulips in beds and borders, on rockeries or in containers. Soil should be well drained with a high organic content. Add lime to acid soils.

GROWING METHOD

Planting   Bulbs should be planted in late autumn. Planting depth varies according to the size of the bulbs; usually 15–20cm (6–8in) for the larger types and 10cm (4in) for the smaller species. Space them 10–20cm (4–8in) apart.

Feeding   Apply liquid fertiliser as soon as buds appear and again after flowers have faded. Water regularly in dry spells, especially once the buds have appeared.

Problems   Tulip breaking virus, causing streaking of the flowers, is carried by aphids. Remove affected plants and keep aphids under control. Tulip fire disease is a type of botrytis or grey mould. It causes small brown spots on flowers and leaves; stems may rot and grey furry growth may develop on the damaged areas. Destroy plants infected with this disease and avoid planting tulips in the same spot for a couple of years. Spraying with a general fungicide may control early infection.

FLOWERING

Season   Tulips flower somewhere between late winter and late spring, depending on variety.

Cutting   If cutting blooms for the house, choose those that are not fully open and cut them early in the morning. Change vase water frequently.

AFTER FLOWERING

Requirements   Remove spent flower stems and dead foliage. Tulips may be left in the ground for two or three years, or the bulbs can be lifted once the foliage has died down, cleaned and stored in a cool, dry, airy place. Dwarf tulips tend to be left in the ground, but other varieties usually perform better if they are lifted and replanted every year. If you do not want to lift them annually, make sure the bulbs are planted deeply.

TULIPA AT A GLANCE

Well-known flowers in a very wide range of colours, sizes and forms, flowering between late winter and late spring.

Month		RECOMMENDED VARIETIES
JAN	/	
FEB	flowering	'Peach Blossom'
MAR	flowering	'Apeldoorn'
APR	flowering	'Clara Butt'
MAY	flowering	'China Pink'
JUN	/	'Burgundy Lace'
JULY	/	'Spring Green'
AUG	/	'Texas Gold'
SEPT	/	'Angelique'
OCT	/	'Ancilla'
NOV	plant	*Tulipa fosteriana*
DEC	plant	*Tulipa greigii*
		Tulipa tarda

TULIPS
(*TULIPA*)

Tulips, with their wide range of forms and colours, are divided into fifteen horticultural groups.

1. From a crimson bud 'Leen van der Mark' opens to reveal a crystalline white centre.

2. A fully opened 'Bokassa Red' shows its deep scarlet petals tipped with gold.

3. 'Judith Lyster', a single late tulip, is rich cream merging to watermelon pink.

4. Goblet-shaped 'Bokassa Rose' is deep rose pink with a yellow centre.

5. 'Kees Nelis' is a bright, two-tone tulip in primary red and yellow.

6. No two parrot tulip flowers are identical as this flamboyant 'Flaming Parrot' proves.

7. 'Princess Victoria' is a heavy-textured tulip that is more weather resistant than some other varieties.

8. 'Angélique', a pale pink ruffled beauty, is best grown in pots so it can be protected from weather.

9. 'Monte Carlo' is a bright gold, fully double tulip with a light scent.

4.

5.

8.

9.

1.

2.

3.

6.

7.

TULIPA
Tulip

THE POINTED PETALS of these goblet-shaped, bright lipstick-pink tulips will open to form a starry shape.

A NATIVE of Crete, pale pink Tulipa saxatilis *needs a sunny, warm position with perfectly drained soil in which to grow.*

FEATURES

There are over 100 species of tulips and many hundreds of hybrids. Most modern garden tulips are the result of extensive breeding programmes that began in the late sixteenth century in Europe and are continuing to this day. Tulips were all the rage at that time as more and more species were introduced to Europe from Turkey, Iran and central Asia. Tulip species range in height from about 15–60cm (6–24in) but the greatest number of hybrids are probably in the range of 30–40cm (12–16in). Tulips look their best in mass plantings of one colour but they can, of course, be mixed. They make very good container plants and are delightful cut flowers. Some of the most charming are the dwarf types which do particularly well in rock gardens and are also very suitable for containers.

Tulip bulbs are widely available in garden centres in late summer and early autumn, but to get a wider choice it is often best to obtain catalogues from specialist bulb growers who run mail-order businesses. Many of the species tulips are only available from specialist growers. With careful selection it is possible to have a tulip in flower from early to very late spring.

Like daffodils, tulips are split into a number of divisions according to their flower form and time of flowering.

Single early	Cup-shaped single flowers, up to 40cm (16in) in early to mid-spring.
Double early	Fully double flowers up to 40cm (16in) in early to mid-spring.
Triumph	Conical then rounded, single flowers up to 50cm (20in) in mid to late spring.
Darwin hybrid	Large, single flowers of varying shape, up to 60cm (24in) in mid to late spring.
Single late	Single, blocky or square shaped flowers up to 75cm (30in) in late spring and early summer.
Lily-flowered	Single, waisted flowers with pointed petals, up to 60cm (24in) in late spring.
Fringed	Single flowers with very finely cut petal edges, up to 60cm (24in) in late spring.
Viridiflora	Single flowers with green bands or streaks on the outside, up to 50cm (20in) in late spring.
Rembrandt	Single flowers with a broken pattern of feathering or streaking caused by a virus. Up to 75cm (30in) in late spring.
Parrot	Single flowers with very strongly frilled and curled petals, up to 60cm (24in) in late spring.
Double late	Large, fully double flowers up to 60cm (24in) in late spring.
Kaufmanniana	Single, often bi-coloured flowers of a waterlily shape, up to 25cm (10in) in late spring. Leaves may be mottled.
Fosteriana	Large, single, wide-opening flowers up to 50cm (20in) in early to mid-spring.
Greigii	Large, single flowers up to 35cm (14in) in mid to late spring. Leaves streaked and mottled.
Miscellaneous	Any other species, varieties and hybrids.

Continued on page 104

WATSONIA
Watsonia

THE VIVID PINK FLOWERS *of watsonia make it a most desirable plant, but it is not commonly grown in gardens.*

WATSONIA FLOWERS *are displayed well clear of the upright foliage and so are ideal for planting at the back of a border.*

FEATURES

Although there are many species of watsonias in the wild, they are not commonly cultivated plants. The stiff, sword-shaped leaves are similar to those of a gladiolus: the flower spike, growing to over 1m (39in) carries tubular flowers in various shades of pink and red, violet, magenta and orange. Watsonia is ideally placed towards the back of a mixed border. In all but very warm districts the corms should be lifted in autumn and stored in a dry place until it is time to replant them the following spring.

The usual species offered is *W. pillansii* (also known as *W. beatricis*), which has orange-red flowers. The slightly more tender *W. borbonica* (*W. pyrimidata*) has rich pink blooms.

WATSONIA AT A GLANCE

An unusual bulb with tall, stately spikes of pink or red flowers, good for the back of the border.

		RECOMMENDED VARIETIES
JAN	/	
FEB	/	
MAR	/	
APR	plant	'Stanford Scarlet'
MAY	plant	'Tresco Dwarf Pink'
JUN	flowering	
JULY	flowering	*Watsonia borbonica ardernei*
AUG	flowering	
SEPT	plant (warm areas)	
OCT	/	
NOV	/	
DEC	/	

CONDITIONS

Aspect   Watsonia needs full sun and a warm, sheltered position.

Site   These tall plants are good for the back of a border. They can also be grown in pots in a greenhouse. Any well-drained soil is acceptable, but growth will be better if well-rotted organic matter is dug in before planting.

GROWING METHOD

Planting   Plant corms in mid to late spring, 10cm (4in) deep and 30cm (12in) apart. In warm, sheltered areas, corms can be planted in autumn 15cm (6in) deep and mulched with chipped bark or dry leaves.

Feeding   Apply a long-acting fertiliser such as general fertiliser in early summer. Watering is necessary only in prolonged dry spells.

Problems   Generally free from pest or disease problems when grown in an open, sunny position.

FLOWERING

Season   Watsonias flower in mid-summer.

Cutting   Stems can be cut for the vase. They should last well with frequent water changes.

AFTER FLOWERING

Requirements Except in very warm areas, lift the corms after flowering, when the foliage starts to die down. Clean them, allow them to dry, and store in a cool, airy place until the following spring.

ZANTEDESCHIA

Arum lily, calla lily

ARUM LILIES have long been favourites with flower arrangers for their texture and sculptural shape which adds form to an arrangement.

PURE WHITE FLOWERS and decorative leaves are features of arum, which are quite easy to grow in a variety of conditions.

FEATURES

Arum lilies are greatly prized for their beautiful waxy flowers, pure white with a golden central spadix. The arrow-shaped leaves are deep green, and the whole plant can grow up to 1m (39in) high. Several species are suitable for growing only in a greenhouse or conservatory, but *Z. aethiopica* can be grown outside in reasonably sheltered gardens. It likes moist, boggy conditions, and often grows best beside a pond or water feature: it can be grown as a marginal plant in up to 30cm (12in) of water. *Z. elliottiana*, the golden arum, and *Z. rehmannii*, the pink arum, are good greenhouse or conservatory plants.

ZANTEDESCHIA AT A GLANCE

A rhizomatous plant grown for its beautiful waxy white flower spathes. Needs greenhouse conditions in some areas.

		RECOMMENDED VARIETIES
JAN	/	
FEB	/	*Zantedeschia aethiopica:*
MAR	/	'Crowborough'
APR	plant ✍	'Green Goddess'
MAY	/	
JUN	flowering ✿	
JULY	flowering ✿	
AUG	/	
SEPT	/	
OCT	/	
NOV	/	
DEC	/	

CONDITIONS

Aspect Can be grown in full sun or light shade. It should be sheltered from strong wind.

Site *Z. aethiopica* can be grown on the fringe of a pool or in a border in moist, humus-rich soil. Other arum species need rich but free-draining soil and are grown in a greenhouse or conservatory in containers.

GROWING METHOD

Planting Plant rhizomes 15cm (6in) deep and 45cm (18in) apart in spring.

Feeding Apply liquid fertiliser as buds appear and continue to feed every 14–21 days while plants are in bloom. Keep the soil moist at all times while the plants are in active growth during spring and summer.

Problems Leaf spot can cause dark blotches on all parts of the plant and may cause premature leaf drop. It often occurs where conditions are too cool and damp. Destroy affected parts and spray with a suitable fungicide.

FLOWERING

Season Flowers in early summer.

Cutting Flowers are excellent for cutting.

AFTER FLOWERING

Requirements Remove flower stems as they fade. Mulch outdoor plants with dry leaves for winter.

ZEPHYRANTHES
Zephyr lily, rainflower

ZEPHYR LILY *shows how even the simplest of flowers can be very beautiful. The green throat and yellow stamens emphasise the purity.*

A BROAD BORDER *of zephyr lily gives a star-studded performance in the autumn garden.*

FEATURES

With its starry white flowers and shiny green, grass-like foliage, zephyr lily is a bulb for mass planting in sheltered gardens. It is quite easy to grow and can remain undisturbed for years where conditions suit it. It can be planted in borders or on a rockery, and it can also be grown very successfully in containers. The crocus-like flowers are carried in late summer or autumn, especially after showers of rain, which accounts for its common name of rainflower.

Zephyranthes candida is the species suitable for growing outdoors in Britain; it generally reaches a height of 20–25cm (8–10in).

Z. grandiflora (also called *Z. rosea*) has lovely rosy pink flowers but is only suitable for cultivation in a greenhouse or conservatory, as is the yellow flowered *Z. citrina*.

ZEPHYRANTHES AT A GLANCE

An attractive, low-growing plant with crocus-like flowers in autumn.

		RECOMMENDED SPECIES
JAN	/	
FEB	/	*Zephyranthes candida*
MAR	/	
APR	plant	*Z. citrina*
MAY	/	
JUN	flowering *	*Z. flavissima*
JULY	flowering *	
AUG	/	*Z. grandiflora*
SEPT	flowering	
OCT	flowering	
NOV	/	
DEC	/	

* indoors

CONDITIONS

Aspect Grows best in full sun.
Site Grow in beds or borders or in pockets in a rockery. Needs a well-drained but moisture-retentive soil. Growth will be improved if soils contain some humus.

GROWING METHOD

Planting Plant in spring, 5cm (2in) deep and 10cm (4in) apart. For greenhouse cultivation, plant 5 bulbs in a 12.5cm (5in) pot in loam-based potting compost.
Feeding Supplementary fertiliser is generally not needed. Spread a mulch of well-decayed manure or compost around the bulbs in spring. Water in dry spells during spring, but stop watering when the foliage starts to die down.
Problems No specific problems are usually experienced with this plant.

FLOWERING

Season Flowers appear from late summer into autumn, or in mid-summer in the greenhouse.
Cutting Flowers are not suitable for cutting.

AFTER FLOWERING

Requirements Spent flower stems may be cut off but this is not essential. No special treatment is needed as the bulbs are best left undisturbed for several years. If you wish to lift and divide a clump this is best done in spring. Greenhouse plants should be allowed to dry out when the leaves die down, and started into growth again by plentiful watering the following spring.

PLANT NAME	SPRING			SUMMER			AUTUMN			WINTER		
	EARLY	MID	LATE	EARLY	MID	LATE	EARLY	MID	LATE	EARLY	MID	LATE
Achimenes				❀	❀	❀	❀					
Agapanthus					❀	❀	❀					
Allium			❀	❀	❀	❀						
Alstroemeria				❀	❀	❀						
Amaryllis belladonna							❀	❀				
Anemone	❀	❀	❀	❀	❀	❀						❀
Anomatheca					❀	❀	❀					
Begonia					❀	❀	❀					
Camassia			❀	❀	❀	❀						
Canna					❀	❀	❀					
Chionodoxa	❀	❀										❀
Clivia	❀	❀										❀
Colchicum							❀	❀	❀			
Convallaria		❀	❀									
Crinum						❀	❀					
Crocosmia					❀	❀	❀					
Crocus	❀	❀					❀	❀	❀		❀	❀
Cyclamen	❀	❀					❀	❀	❀	❀	❀	❀
Cyrtanthus					❀	❀	❀					
Dahlia					❀	❀	❀	❀				
Dierama					❀	❀	❀					
Eranthis	❀	❀										❀
Eremurus				❀	❀							
Erythronium		❀	❀									
Eucomis					❀	❀						
Freesia	❀					❀	❀	❀			❀	❀
Fritillaria		❀	❀									
Galanthus	❀	❀									❀	❀
Gladiolus			❀	❀	❀	❀	❀					
Gloriosa					❀	❀	❀					
Hedychium					❀	❀						
Hippeastrum	❀	❀									❀	❀
Hyacinthoides		❀	❀									

PLANT NAME	SPRING			SUMMER			AUTUMN			WINTER		
	EARLY	MID	LATE	EARLY	MID	LATE	EARLY	MID	LATE	EARLY	MID	LATE
Hyacinthus	✽	✽								✽	✽	✽
Hymenocallis			✽	✽		✽	✽					
Ipheion	✽	✽	✽									
Iris	✽	✽	✽	✽	✽			✽	✽	✽	✽	✽
Ixia			✽	✽	✽							
Lachenalia	✽										✽	✽
Leucojum	✽	✽	✽				✽					✽
Lilium				✽	✽	✽	✽					
Moraea				✽	✽	✽						
Muscari	✽	✽	✽									
Narcissus	✽	✽	✽	✽							✽	✽
Nerine							✽	✽	✽			
Ornithogalum		✽	✽	✽	✽							
Oxalis				✽	✽							
Polianthes						✽	✽	✽				
Ranunculus				✽	✽	✽						
Rhodohypoxis			✽	✽	✽	✽	✽					
Romulea	✽	✽	✽									
Schizostylis							✽	✽	✽			
Scilla	✽	✽	✽	✽								✽
Sinningia				✽	✽	✽						
Sparaxis			✽	✽								
Sprekelia				✽								
Sternbergia							✽	✽				
Tigridia						✽	✽					
Trillium		✽	✽	✽								
Triteleia			✽	✽	✽							
Tritonia			✽	✽								
Tulbaghia				✽	✽	✽						
Tulipa	✽	✽	✽									✽
Watsonia				✽	✽	✽						
Zantedeschia				✽	✽							
Zephyranthes				✽	✽		✽	✽				

INDEX

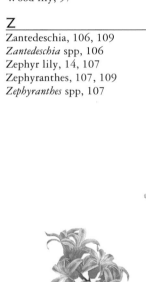

Published by Murdoch Books UK Ltd, 1998
Ferry House, 51-57 Lacy Road, Putney, London SW15 1PR

This edition published 2001 for INDEX: Henson Way,
Kettering, NN16 8PX, United Kingdom

Text copyright © Murdoch Books UK Ltd
Photography copyright © Murdoch Books (except those listed below)

ISBN 1-897730-92-6

First published 1998. Reprinted 2001. Printed by Toppan in China.

A catalogue of this book is available from the British Library.

Series Editor: Graham Strong

Editor: Jane Courtier

Text: Margaret Hanks

Illustrations: Sonya Naumov

Designers: Karen Awadzi, Annette Fitzgerald and Jackie Richards

Managing Editor: Christine Eslick

Commissioning Editor: Helen Griffin

Publisher: Anne Wilson

Photographs: All photographs by Lorna Rose except those by Stirling Macoboy (pp27L and R, 99, 97R);
Reg Morrison (pp62-63, 78-79, 80-81, 72L, 102-103);
Graham Strong (pp2-3, 22R, 29, 31R, 40, 47L and R, 53R, 66L and R, 67R, 90R);
Eric Sawford (pp23L, 36R, 37R, 45L, 49R, 51, 54R, 67L);
Harry Smith (pp20R, 26L, 28R, 92R);
International Flower Bulb Centre (pp31L, 46 L and R, 55L, 74L, 92L);
Pat Brindley (pp32R, 76L, 96R);
Photos Horticultural (pp39R, 52R, 53R);
Gerry Whitmont (p75L);
and S & O Matthews (pp45R and 73R).

Front cover: Pink and yellow tulips with purple hyacinths